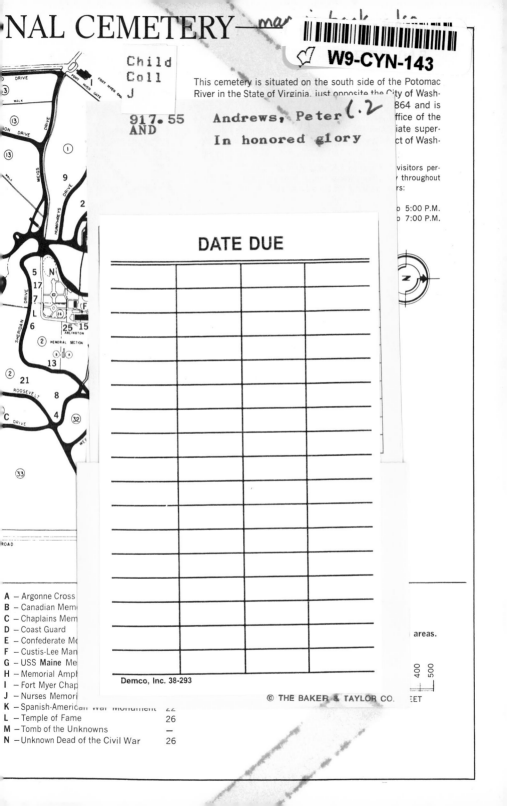

NAL CEMETERY—

Andrews, Peter l.2

In honored glory

This cemetery is situated on the south side of the Potomac River in the State of Virginia, just opposite the City of Wash- ...864 and is ...ffice of the ...iate super- ...ct of Wash-

...visitors per- ...throughout ...rs:

...5:00 P.M.
...7:00 P.M.

DATE DUE

© THE BAKER & TAYLOR CO.

areas.

400 500

...ET

A – Argonne Cross
B – Canadian Mem...
C – Chaplains Mem...
D – Coast Guard
E – Confederate M...
F – Custis-Lee Man...
G – USS Maine Me...
H – Memorial Amph...
I – Fort Myer Chap...
J – Nurses Memori...
K – Spanish-American War Monument 22
L – Temple of Fame 26
M – Tomb of the Unknowns —
N – Unknown Dead of the Civil War 26

IN HONORED GLORY

IN
HONORED
GLORY

THE STORY OF ARLINGTON

By Peter Andrews

G. P. PUTNAM'S SONS
NEW YORK

CONTENTS

IN HONORED GLORY

I

THIS HALLOWED GROUND

AND still they come—8,000 a day—the mourners, the dignitaries from foreign states, the merely curious, the
deeply awed.

The grave site of the late President John F. Kennedy, still
as unfinished as his political aspirations and programs, not
yet commemorated in the monumental trappings of marble
and statuary, has already become a national shrine with
unique appeal. It is a place of honor and wonder: wonder
that a nation could produce so ebullient a man, so charismatic a leader. It is a place of shame: shame that the same
nation could produce the man who so casually struck him
down.

The people come at all times of the day to perform their
numb rituals. Strangely somber schoolchildren are brought
by school bus with their religious medals to leave at the
site. Businessmen come in taxis during their lunch break as
if they half expected the grave were all a mistake and that
it would be gone when they returned. Soldiers file by and
following the time-honored custom of the military, leave
their campaign hats on the grave of the fallen commander.

Beside the grave is a clutch of shamrocks brought over from Ireland and planted there by the Irish Ambassador with Mrs. Kennedy. Italian President Segni laid on a small, faded nosegay that had been made by an Italian peasant woman and tenderly carried across the sea. At night, the late President's brother, Senator Robert Kennedy, comes to kneel at the site and ponder into the blue flame that burns eternally on the site.

Along Meigs Road nearby comes the chilled clatter of horses' hooves on the pavement as the perpetually busy work of tending to the dead goes on. This time there are no masses of mourners: no television to follow the cortège of a national figure, no platoons of officers and men, no bands, no riderless horse with stirrups in reverse, no artillery barrages nor lines of pallbearers.

A squad of men, a single bugler, a chaplain and a soldier's widow trailing behind the horse-drawn caisson are enough to do a man honor.

The procession stops by a prepared site and the chaplain repeats the old words:

"Man, that is born of woman, hath but a short time to live, and is full of misery. He cometh up, and is cut down like a flower; he fleeth as it were a shadow and never continueth in one stay.

"In the midst of life we are in death. . . ."

As the coffin is lowered into the ground, the flag that has covered it is removed and folded into a triangular form and handed to the widow. There is the sound of three sharp volleys of rifle fire and then after a moment of stillness the bugle sounds taps.

As an excursion bus lumbers along on its way toward the Memorial Bridge to take its passengers on to the next scene of interest, another funeral procession gets under way. There will be two dozen like it before the day is out.

This then, is Arlington Cemetery, just across the Potomac River from Washington, D.C. Officially, Arlington is part of a series of national cemeteries operated by the United States Army. In actual fact, the grounds of Arlington are the most complete and perhaps the only direct physical link with America's turbulent past.

There are more than 120,000 men and women buried at Arlington. It is the last resting place for veterans of every American military action since, and including, the Revolution. Its almost 420 acres hold more of the history of the Republic and the men who made it than any other place in the world.

A reflective tour of its ten miles of curving thoroughfares is a capsule history of America.

Men and memorials—that is the spirit of Arlington.

Buried here are Presidents Taft and Kennedy; Secretaries of State George Marshall and John Foster Dulles; Generals Phil Sheridan, John Pershing and Claire Chennault; Admirals Robert Peary, Richard Byrd and "Bull" Halsey. Erected here are memorials to men who flew the oceans, to women who tended soldiers under fire, to those who simply went out and died because their country said their sacrifice was needed.

Three veterans of the Revolution are here. Fourteen slain in the War of 1812 are here also, all of them unknown. Almost 18,000 graves from the Civil War are here. Along with them are the first of the towering monuments put up by a grieving nation. There is a simple but massive granite vault containing the bodies of 2,111 unknown soldiers recovered from the battlefields of Bull Run and along the Rappahannock. There is the giant Confederate Monument, placed in 1914 to commemorate a reunited North and South, which watches over the graves of some 500 Confederate dead interred in Arlington.

Standing sentinel along with the dogwood trees and massive oaks of Arlington is the mast of USS *Maine* which honors those who perished when she was sunk in Havana harbor, prior to the Spanish-American War.

From World War I came more graves and more monuments. The Tomb of the Unknown Soldier and the classic Memorial Amphitheatre are, by far, the most impressive sights at Arlington. The Tomb, near the old Custis-Lee mansion that once belonged to Robert E. Lee, looks broodingly down the rolling hill toward Washington. Its inscription etches on the mind as clearly as it does on the pure white Colorado marble:

> Here Rests In
> Honored Glory
> An American
> Soldier
> Known But to God

The amphitheatre is at once a memorial in itself to men who died in battle, and a magnificent outdoor setting for religious ceremonies.

The sacrifice of World War II and Korea is seen here also. The majestic Tomb of the Unknown Soldier is flanked by unknown dead of these two conflicts.

As the styles and manners of America have changed, so has Arlington. The impressive and sometimes cluttered personal monuments of 40 years ago are no longer permitted. In their place are the neat Government-regulation headstones laid in symmetric row upon row. There has been a drawing together of men even in death at Arlington. A solitary rococo headstone with the flamboyant poetry that appealed to generals of the Civil War would not have been in an Army-regulation headstone with the men of the AEF.

As man's ability to destroy himself in greater numbers increases, he leaves the signs of efficiency in the mass graves of Arlington. The largest from World War II contains the bodies of 250 men who died together off Lunga Beach in Guadalcanal when the USS *Serpens* exploded and went to the bottom. Tank and plane crews who perished as a unit are buried together.

General of the Army Douglas MacArthur once said:

"The soldier, above all other men, is required to perform the highest act of religious sacrifice. In battle and in the face of danger and death he discloses those divine attributes which his Maker gave when He created man in His own image. No physical courage and no brute instincts can take the place of the annunciation and spiritual uplift which will alone sustain him. However horrible the incidents of war may be, the soldier who is called upon to offer and to give his life for his country is one of the noblest developments of mankind. I do not know the dignity of his birth, but I do know the glory of his death."

The following pages are an attempt to tell some of the story of this place and these men—how Arlington came to mean what it does and who some of these men were and what they did. They all have one thing in common. They served. There is no higher calling.

II

THE SEIZURE

ON April 12, 1861, cannonade from shore batteries plowed into the United States Government Army post of Fort Sumter in South Carolina and the climactic issue of American history was finally joined by force of arms. Six days later, Colonel Robert E. Lee was summoned into the office of the United States commanding general, Winfield Scott, to be offered a loaded pistol.

This was a time for choosing, and perhaps nowhere was the choice more agonizing than for the United States military officers from the state of Virginia. A border state, Virginia was more deeply divided on the subject of secession than most of the South. The officers born in Virginia, some of the very best fighting men of the war, reflected that division. Winfield Scott, the great national hero since the war of 1812, and the historically underrated General George Thomas remained staunchly for the Union. Joe Johnston, Jubal Early, John Magruder and Thomas "Stonewall" Jackson all offered their swords to their native state. Most important to the future conduct of the war was the decision of Robert E. Lee, a brevet colonel in the Corps of Engineers who had distinguished himself by personal valor and a sure hand for the complexities of command during the Mexican campaigns. Lee was the personal choice of Scott to take command of the Federal forces.

On April 17, the Virginia convention voted an ordinance of secession. Lee would have to decide between his state and his country. Neither a slaver nor a secessionist, Lee was loath to see the Union split but was even more disenchanted with the idea that a Union established by consent could be kept together by force.

"I can anticipate no greater calamity for the country than the dissolution of the Union," he wrote shortly before the full fury of the war broke loose. "Still a Union that can only be maintained by swords and bayonets and in which strife and civil war are to take the place of brotherly love has no charms for me."

Scott tried to force Lee's hand the day after the Virginia convention's vote. He offered him the command of the Federal armies, specifically the Army of the Potomac. By offering Lee the highest command available, Scott had hoped to ensure that the services of the country's leading soldier would be available to the Union. Lee refused, and retired to his home, Arlington, across the Potomac, to contemplate his next move.

The mansion, then as now, was an unmistakable landmark on the Washington scene. Built in the early 1800's the Arlington house was an almost perfect example of the Greek Revival style that was so often sought after and so rarely captured during that period of American architectural development. Situated on a prominent knoll on a 1,100-acre estate, Arlington was one of the great showplaces along the river. Its monumental columns, which seem overly large to someone standing near them, were designed for their visual effect on a visitor approaching from the other side of the Potomac.

In addition to the natural beauty of its site and the grandeur of its appointments, Arlington also served as the chief repository of mementoes of President George Washington. The property was originally owned by John Parke Custis, the only son of Martha Washington by her first marriage. John died of camp fever while serving as an aide to General Washington at Yorktown. The general adopted John's young son, George Washington Parke Custis, and took him to Mount Vernon. John had never had the chance to build a house on his property. On his own, following the deaths of George Washington in 1799 and Martha in 1802, the twenty-two-year-old George Custis undertook building a country home on his father's property that could house the vast amount of memorabilia he had inherited and brought from the Washington estate.

Slowly, over the years, Custis developed the Arlington mansion. In the style of the day, he built the wings first and then joined them with the spacious central section.

One of the few Virginia families that could match the social prominence and historical lineage of the Custises were the heirs of the great Revolutionary figure and former governor of the state, General "Light-Horse Harry" Lee. Both families looked on approvingly as their children, young Mary Custis and Lieutenant Robert E. Lee, courted and were finally engaged. The couple were married in the main living room at the Arlington mansion.

After Custis died, the house and property passed on to the fragile Mary, whose chronic ill health made her a partial invalid, and Robert E. Lee became the master of the Arlington estate. It became a place, he once remarked, "where my affections and attachments are more strongly placed than any other place in the world."

When Lee rode up to his beloved house on the evening of Friday, April 19, after refusing command of the Federal armies, there were a group of friends waiting to hear from him what he planned to do next. He had refused the command, but would he stay with the Union? Would he fight for the South? Would he fight at all? Lee excused himself and walked in the garden that he and his wife cultivated with such care. Lee used to make it a ritual when the roses were in bloom to cut one for each of his daughters and put them at their places at the breakfast table. He returned and went upstairs. The group sitting downstairs could hear him as he paced in his bedroom and as he knelt to pray. Sometime after midnight, he sat down and penned a note to General Scott resigning his commission.

"Save in the defense of my native state, I never desire again to draw my sword."

He went downstairs and told his wife, "Well, Mary, the question is settled."

Lee knew the tactical implications of what his decision would mean to the property located so close to the capital and must have assumed it would be occupied by Federal troops if he went through with his plan to join the cause of the South. The horses were ready early Monday morning. Lee did not linger, and set straight for Richmond to accept a commission in the Rebel army. He never again set foot on Arlington. Except for a glimpse of the property from a passing railroad train years after the war was over he never saw it again.

Before he left, Lee had pleaded with his wife to seek the

safety of Richmond but at first she seemed not to understand the situation. It was not until the next month that she began to make preparations to evacuate her family and pack up their belongings. As it was, Mrs. Lee just had time to throw some of the paintings and a small portion of the more valuable silver on wagons and leave before a detachment of Union cavalry clattered over the Potomac bridge and seized the Arlington heights. As a result of the confusion in the hasty evacuation many priceless heirlooms of the George Washington family were lost, some forever.

Trenches and earthworks were thrown up along the rambling paths of Arlington, and Union officers and men were headquartered in the house itself.

The next year the wheels were set in motion that would turn Arlington into Government property and eventually into one of America's most beautiful and cherished national shrines. Arlington's transformation was to begin on the tawdriest of notes. It was stolen.

The first step seemed innocuous enough. Congress passed and President Lincoln signed an omnibus bill, one provision of which held that "the President of the United States shall have power, whenever in his opinion it shall be expedient, to purchase cemetery grounds and cause them to be securely enclosed to be used as a national cemetery for the soldiers who shall die in the service of the country."

As a result of this edict, national burial grounds were established in nearby Alexandria, Virginia, and also on the grounds of the Old Soldiers' Home in the District of Columbia.

Before the war had begun, General Winfield Scott laid out what was called the "Anaconda Plan." It was a tragically accurate forecast of how the war would be waged. It foresaw an extended conflict requiring lengthy training periods, full national mobilization, and a maximum effort by the entire North. It was a good plan, but no one believed it, and Scott, aging and suffering from dropsy, was dismissed as a doddering incompetent. Political leaders clung to the belief that all that would be needed was to dispatch a force southward and be done with it. Ignorant amateur armies rushed out into the country and perished by the thousands learning new tactics in the ancient art of war.

As there had been no adequate preparations for fighting the gigantic war that was to engulf the Republic, there had been not even minimal preparations to handle the masses of dead. When they were buried at all, men were buried where they died. On the battlefields of Antietam, Fredericksburg and Chancellorsville they were often just left to nature. In overcrowded hospitals the burial details became common scandals.

As a result of a popular outcry, Lincoln ordered Secretary of War Edwin Stanton to secure additional burial ground in the Washington area. Stanton turned the job over to his hardworking and able quartermaster general, Montgomery Meigs, and told him to make a survey of likely spots. Under this precedent, the duty of supervising the national burial grounds remains a duty of the Quartermaster Corps.

It was a job ideally suited to Meigs. He already had the location selected and he had a vengeful turn of mind to do something about it.

Two years before, in 1862, the Government had seized the Lee property at Arlington on a slippery charge of delinquent taxes. Under an 1862 law concerning "the collection of direct taxes in insurrectionary districts within the United States," the Lee property was declared forfeit to the Government because of a tax bill of $92.07. When Mrs. Lee tried to pay the tax bill through a cousin, the Federal Government refused to accept payment on the grounds that the invalid wife of the Southern general would have to cross through the combat lines and come to Washington to pay the taxes in person. When she did not, the Government seized the property.

There is no direct evidence that Meigs was personally behind this procedure, but his hand is clearly seen in the rest of the story of Arlington. Whether through personal vengeance because of some real or imagined slight from Lee, or whether, in a real sense, Meigs considered Lee to be an arch-traitor to the Republic, he took time off from the war to personally destroy Arlington forever as a suitable site for a home.

After the seizure, Meigs engineered a closed auction of the Arlington property. The Lee estate, originally taken to pay off a $92.07 tax bill was put on the auctioneer's block at the assessed price of $26,810 for all 1,100 acres and the buildings. The Government was the only bidder allowed at the auction, and as a result it secured the entire property, buildings and all, for the exact assessed value.

According to official records the property was reserved "for Government use, for war, military, charitable and educational purposes."

Stanton had told Meigs to inspect several possibilities for a burial site around the Washington area, and report back with as many recommendations as he wished to make. Meigs was back at Stanton's desk the next day with only one recommendation—Arlington.

It is not reported whether Stanton had any misgivings about the propriety or the legality of the act. Probably not.

The need for burial space was great, and what better place than in the lawns of the hero of the South. On June 15, 1864, Stanton signed an order authorizing the use of 200 acres around the main house as burial space.

He need not have bothered. Without waiting for any authorization, Meigs had ordered the burials to begin a month before the Stanton order. On May 13, Private William Christman, Company G of the 67th Pennsylvania Infantry, was interred in Arlington. Dozens, then hundreds, then thousands were to follow, including Montgomery Meigs, who preselected for himself and his family a choice pair of sites near the Lee mansion.

Meigs had planned to surround the Lee home with graves so that it would be all but unapproachable from then on. This started a grisly tug of war between Meigs and the officers quartered in the main house.

Burial details brought bodies up to Arlington to be buried near the house. As they arrived, the officers, who did not take kindly to the thought of being encircled by fresh graves, ordered the burial details to take their cargoes and bury them as far away on the property as possible.

When Meigs came out to Arlington in August of that year to check on his handiwork he was furious. Instead of seeing the Lee house ringed with graves, he saw the mansion looking much as it always had, except for the troops lounging about and taking their ease. Down toward the orchard near the old slave quarters was a neat looking cemetery filled with all of the bodies Meigs had wanted placed near the house. Enraged, he ordered twenty-six more bodies brought over from Washington right away, and in the hot August sun, Major General Montgomery Meigs, Quartermaster General of the United States Army, stood by and personally supervised their burial in the rose garden just south of the house.

No Lee ever again lived in Arlington. General Lee himself made several attempts to regain the home for his wife, but he died in 1870 before anything could be done. His son, General George Washington Custis Lee, took the battle up to the Supreme Court. In 1882 the high court ruled that Arlington did indeed rightfully belong to the Lee family. The Government and its cemetery facility were adjudged to be trespassers. In lieu of actually repossessing the property, Lee settled with the Government for $150,000 as full payment.

The settlement came too late for Mrs. Lee, who died in 1873, three years after her husband passed away. She had gone back to Arlington only once after the war. Her carriage drove up the winding pathways she had taken so many times as a child in a pony cart. As the carriage stopped in front of her former home, she saw a paper sign tacked by the front door reading

GOVERNMENT PROPERTY
KEEP OUT

Mrs. Lee sat in the carriage without attempting to get out. An old Negro servant who had worked for the Lees before the war, recognized her and offered her a drink of cool water from the well. Mrs. Lee drank the water, thanked him, and told the carriage driver to take her away. She never looked back.

III

A COUNTRY CEMETERY
BECOMES A NATIONAL SHRINE

THE site of Arlington Cemetery had started as a throw-together expedient to handle the needs of the local Washington area. Within a year it became the national burying ground for the Republic. On August 6, 1866, the bodies of 2,111 unknown soldiers recovered from the battlefields at Bull Run and along the route to the Rappahannock were brought to Arlington and buried with a single monument in Section 26. These were the first combat Unknowns put in Arlington.*

James Parks,** a slave born on the old Arlington property, who stayed on as a maintenance man and grave digger, once said he remembered the early days of the cemetery when the bodies of Union soldiers were brought in for burial by the thousands and were "piled up like cordwood" by the side of the old Lee mansion.

---

* Eventually there were 11,911 known and 5,349 unknown bodies from the Civil War buried in Arlington. These figures include men and women from both the North and the South.

** Parks lived to be more than 100 years old and died in 1929. In his will he asked to be buried in Arlington, where he had spent his entire life. Although he was not eligible, special permission was granted by the Government.

The first moves to establish a day of national remembrance came in 1868 when General John A. Logan, Commander in Chief of the Grand Army of the Republic, selected May 30 as a day to be set aside for "strewing with flowers or otherwise decorating the graves of comrades who died in defense of their country . . . and other fitting services and testimonials of respect."

The first Memorial Day service in Arlington was a great procession which came across the same bridge that the detachment of Union cavalry had used to seize the old Custis-Lee mansion in the bleak, early days of the war. This time the parade was led by young girls with black satin sashes across their starched white school dresses, bearing flowers and singing "Father Come Home" in high-pitched voices. President Andrew Johnson established a precedent by letting all Government employees off for the day to attend the services. Several thousand streamed to Arlington in the bright spring afternoon to pay their respects to the dead of the Civil War. The procession went first to the grave site of the unknown soldiers who fell at Bull Run and covered it with blossoms and evergreens.

The first Memorial Day set the tone and the traditions that have been followed in small towns and city squares ever since. The assemblage gathered at the base of the flagpole in back of the mansion, its giant pillars all twined in black. There was a prayer. And then a schoolboy, tugging nervously at his trousers, recited the Gettysburg Address. There was a distinguished speaker to deliver some remarks on the nature of sacrifice.

General James A. Garfield was one of the first to realize the inadequacy of words in the silent presence of men cut down in war:

"I am oppressed with a sense of the impropriety of uttering words on this occasion," he said. "If silence is ever golden it must be here beside the graves of fifteen thousand men whose lives were more significant than speech and for whom death was a poem the music of which can never be sung. With words we make promises, plight faith, and praise virtue. Promises may not be kept, plighted faith may be broken and vaunted virtue only the cunning mask of vice. We do not know one promise these men made, one pledge they gave, one word they spoke; but we do know they summoned up and perfected, by one supreme act, the highest virtues of men and citizens. For love of country they accepted death. That act resolved all doubts and made immortal their patriotism and their virtue."

The mourners, led by the schoolgirls and young boys from the soldiers' and sailors' orphanage wearing heavy blue suits, went about the cemetery covering it with flowers.

In 1873 the *Washington Star* declared that "Memorial Day has come to be regarded as one of the most sacred of American commemorative holidays." President Grant appeared in Arlington that year and only ill health has ever kept a President from such services since then.

In those days the sermon was the high point of the service. People loved the florid prose of nineteenth-century church rhetoric.

The Reverend De Witt Talmadge, speaking at the ceremony in 1873, was typical:

"If there be in all this audience a soul so base as to feel no tenderness or thanks let him be gone now and take his polluted foot out of this holy dust," he told the 10,000 who had gathered to hear his remarks. "Walk softly about this place," he warned. "They have gone into the tent for the night, their heads on pillows of dust, their arms stacked, their march ended, their battle fought. Sleep on, great host, till the morning light strikes through the rifts of the tents and the trumpet sounds the reveille of the Resurrection."

Memorial Day at Arlington was a full day's outing for most people. The horses and carriages would begin to arrive early in the morning to get under shade and avoid the heat of noon. Many would pack a lunch and picnic on the grounds. Vendors lined the road leading to Arlington, selling cigars, ice cream, peanuts, soda water and candy. For a penny children could stop at a roadside stand and look at battle scenes of the Civil War through a stereoscopic device.

One vendor set up a lemonade stand right next to the Lee mansion. When business did not live up to his expectations he took the bucket from the well and threw it away. Thirsty people, thundered the *Star*, "were forced to shell out at the rate of five or ten cents per drink for the slops usually sold at such occasions."

By 1897 the physical layout of Arlington was largely set in its present mold. Acreage was added, bringing the cemetery land from the original 200 acres to 408. The slopes overlooking the Potomac east of Arlington were reserved for distinguished officers. South of Meigs Drive was the "Field of the Dead," for enlisted men of the Civil War. The dead of the Rebel cause were buried at Jackson Circle. The grounds in the rear of the mansion toward Fort Myer and to the west were also for Civil War dead of various ranks as well as some civilians. (The dead of the Spanish-American War are for the most part placed along McPherson Drive west of the present Memorial Amphitheatre.) Some 5,000 of those men who were brought back from French battlefield cemeteries were buried below Jackson Circle. The veterans of World War I and II are mostly in the South Grounds.

As more of the nation's heroes were buried in Arlington the cemetery underwent a series of gradual changes. Originally Arlington was supposed to be only for those who died, if not in combat, at least during the duration of the war. Over the years many soldiers requested that they, too, be buried in Arlington. The Government agreed that all soldiers should be made eligible whether they served during wartime or not. Later, Arlington was opened to the immediate families of servicemen. At first Arlington was virtually a potter's field for American military dead. It was quite all right during wartime, but any family of means certainly would not want it known that one of their members had been buried in a Government cemetery during peacetime by choice. If Arlington had not been a military cemetery it would probably have remained a kind of ultimate welfare project. But Washington became the strong Federal Capital of the nation and high-ranking personnel of the armed services came to think of Washington as their home. As a military cemetery, Arlington naturally came to be regarded as their own burial ground, and more and more officers asked to be buried there. With so many of the nation's honored dead already at rest in Arlington, what started as an expedient became sought after as a right of service and the final honor of the soldier.

Early in the morning of February 14, 1898, a shudder went through the plates of the USS *Maine,* moored in Havana Harbor. The ship sank beneath the water, carrying two officers and 251 men with her.* Two months later America became involved in her most criticized foreign venture—the Spanish-American War. Lasting slightly more than 100 days, this "splendid little war" as it has been called, marked the emergence of the United States as a major power on the international scene. It has never been determined whether the explosion was accidental or sabotage, but the monument to the men of the *Maine* (Section 27) is one of the most impressive at Arlington.

There were two separate ceremonies over a thirteen-year period to mark the catastrophe of the *Maine*. Two years after the *Maine* went down, President McKinley and Admiral George Dewey, the hero of the Battle of Manila Bay, stood in the freezing December snow at Arlington to lead a nation of mourners in front of 151 bodies from the stricken *Maine*. All were unidentifiable. The bodies had been buried in the Colon Cemetery in Cuba right after the explosion. They were later exhumed and brought to Arlington for reburial. Each casket was covered with a United States ensign and a storm flag. The ceremonies at the grave sites were brief as each coffin was lowered into the frozen turf.**

President Taft led the nation back to the burial ground of the men of the *Maine* in 1912. The *Maine* itself had been raised in Havana Harbor. Sixty-five bodies, trapped inside

* During the rest of the Spanish-American War only one member of the U.S. Navy was killed in action.

** The ceremonies marked the first recording of the phenomenon that has vexed persons trying to watch important ceremonies ever since—the cameraman. "The omnipresent camera fiend was on hand," remarked the *Washington Star*. "There were seemingly a score of them in fact. During the solemn services they made themselves most obnoxious by snapping pictures from every point of view. While the chaplains were praying, the cameramen were rushing about, setting their machines here and there. Finally several of them intruded actually between the chaplains and the graves and there snapped their Kodaks. They seemed to have absolutely no regard of the meaning and solemnity of the occasion."

the doomed vessel for fourteen years, were taken off and carried back home to America for burial. The mast of the *Maine* was wrenched from the wreckage and brought to Arlington, where it was placed just to the south of the graves of the men who had gone down with her. The names of all who lost their lives in the disaster are inscribed on the base of the memorial.* The *Maine* itself was raised from the muddy harbor bottom and taken out to the open sea and scuttled.

After the turn of the century authorities wanted Arlington to be truly representative of all American conflicts. In 1905 fourteen unknown American soldiers from the War of 1812 were found at the site of the old Washington Barracks near the Treasury and were reinterred in Arlington (Section 1–299).

Between 1907 and 1911 three soldiers from the American Revolution were reinterred. None of them were battle casualties. They are Paymaster Joseph Carlton, John Folin and General James Lingan.

The most towering monument to the sacrifices of the Civil War, the Confederate Monument (Section 16), was put up by the United Daughters of the Confederacy on June 4, 1914. The monument, standing over the graves of some 400 Southern dead buried near there, speaks eloquently of their deaths:

"Not for fame or reward, not for place or for rank, not lured by ambition or goaded by necessity, but in simple obedience to duty as they understood it these men suffered all, sacrificed all, dared all and died."

The dominant figure of the monument is a woman of

---

* The body of the Polish pianist and patriot Jan Paderewski is also entombed inside the *Maine* Monument. Technically Paderewski is not "interred" in Arlington. He is "lying in state" in America and will be returned to his native land when Poland is once again a free nation.

heroic size, symbolizing the South at peace, on top of a series of base-reliefs of 32 figures depicting the heroism of the South at war.*

The great triumph of the Confederate Monument was that it was tangible evidence that the old wounds had begun to heal at last. General Washington Gardner, commander of the Grand Army of the Republic, and General Bennett Young, commander of the United Confederate Veterans, were both cheered as they spoke at the dedication ceremony. Veterans from each side brought wreaths and laid them upon the graves of their old opponents. That night in Washington there was a round of parties for the visitors from both sides of the Mason-Dixon Line.

A young officer, who was born after the Civil War had ended, described the scene saying, "When I saw an old guy from Alabama buying a Pennsylvania Volunteer a drink and swapping lies I knew the war was finally over."

Up until 1915 there was no real gathering place to handle the large crowds that were annually streaming into Arlington for the Memorial Day services. The "amphitheatre" was actually just a place scooped out of the ground. It had no permanent seats.

The surviving members of the GAR were the most active in trying to set a proper amphitheatre for conducting memorial services constructed at Arlington. Ivory Kimball, a GAR officer, went before Congress in 1912 to plead for the structure:

"No one can go there and wander among its monuments to the dead and see the great names on those monuments without being impressed, without having his patriotism

---

* The sculptor, Virginia-born Moses Ezekial, who fought for the Confederacy, died in Italy. In 1921 his remains were removed from Italy and re-interred at the base of the monument.

stirred, without being brought to a higher sense of what the nation means and of what the people of the nation may die for," he said.

"Arlington is not for today; it is not for the Grand Army of the Republic alone; it is not for the Spanish War veterans alone, but during all time as long as this nation lasts Arlington will be unique and will be the burial place of our soldiers."

Then Kimball looked at the faces of the members of the congressional Public Buildings and Grounds Committee and pleaded:

"We are very anxious to have it. . . . We are dying off, gentlemen, we are dying off rapidly and we want to see that building in our day."

Woodrow Wilson laid the cornerstone for the giant Memorial Amphitheatre on October 13, 1915. Modeled chiefly after the Theatre of Dionysus in Athens and a Roman theatre in Orange, France, the amphitheatre was made of white Vermont marble with seats for nearly 5,000 persons in its 200- by 152-foot ellipse. On one side of the amphitheatre is the Lincoln quotation, "Let us here highly resolve that these honored dead shall not have died in vain."

On the other is George Washington's credo, "When we assumed the soldier we did not lay aside the citizen."

On Memorial Day of 1917 the crowds walked through the unfinished amphitheatre* and brought the traditional bowers of flowers to place on the graves. Kindly Southern ladies made it a point to bring blossoms to put on Union graves as well as those of the Confederacy. The gravestones in the Confederate section may have had sharpened triangular points on top. (The story is that they were made that way so

---

* It was finally dedicated in 1920.

"no damn Yankee could sit on them.") Even so, they were covered that day with wreaths graciously sent by the GAR.

A year later American doughboys would be sloshing through the Marne. There would be more graves to decorate in Arlington, but there would never again be a North and a South confronting each other in armed combat.

IV

THE WAR TO END WAR

FRANÇOIS SIMON, an itinerant French painter, had already given one son to the Great War. Now, in 1916, his second son lay gravely wounded.

Simon, himself, was too old to fight. But he did what he could. He had helped organize honorary escorts for burial details to accompany the stream of French dead being borne back from the battlefields to the military cemetery at Rennes.

The large number of nameless crosses at Rennes obsessed Simon. So many sons of France dead with no one to mourn them. So many mothers and fathers who, like himself, had lost a child in the maw of World War I that so voraciously kept demanding more. But, unlike himself, these families had no particular cross to revere—no particular place to mourn. They could only pick their way along the rows and rows of unmarked and unnamed graves and wonder.

As Simon thought about it an idea began to form in his mind, an idea so obvious that it didn't seem really very new. And yet it was so right that within five years each of the four major members of the Allies officially adopted the concept.

Why not make one of the nameless dead soldiers a symbol

for all of the men, known and unknown, who had died for
France? For such a man France could even find room among
the nation's greatest heroes entombed in the Panthéon.

The Chamber of Deputies quickly took to Simon's idea. In
1919 it moved that an unknown French soldier would be
placed in the Panthéon on November 11, 1920, the first anniversary of Armistice Day. The tomb would be marked simply:

Un Soldat
1914 – 19—

Private Auguste Thin, whose father had been killed somewhere on the Western Front, but whose body had never been
recovered, was sent to the cemetery at Verdun, where so
many of the French dead were buried. Thin placed a spray of
red and white carnations on one of the unnamed graves and
the first unknown soldier of World War I was selected. This
nameless soldier was sent back to Paris with honor and glory
that even Napoleon had not been granted.

A few days before the Armistice Day ceremony the French
Parliament decided to heap yet one more honor on its unknown soldier. Instead of being placed in the Panthéon, this
sacred body would be entombed in the Arc de Triomphe
itself.

Paris is normally given to jubilant victory celebrations.
But the city was somber as the soldier's body was borne
through the streets.

As the French hero was being carried to Paris, England was
preparing a similar welcome at Westminster Abbey for an
unknown dead of her own.

A pine field coffin with its precious cargo was lifted from
French soil and placed inside an oaken one with a Crusaders'
sword attached to the lid. With French Marshal Foch and

British Adjutant General Sir George Macdonogh marching behind, the fallen Tommy was taken from a French battlefield cemetery and started home. Under the same Union Jack that had shielded the bodies of the martyred Nurse Edith Cavell and Captain James Fryatt, the body lay in state at Trafalgar Square. A soldier's steel helmet and sidearm were placed on top of the coffin, along with the sword of the Crusaders. King George V knelt to lead his people in mourning on this solemn Armistice Day.

The Union Jack was fanned to the ground, leaving the coffin unadorned except for the simple soldier's tools of war—the helmet, the gun and the sword. At the foot of the coffin lay a state wreath with the inscription written out in the King's own hand:

"In proud memory of those who die unknown in the great war. Unknown and yet well known; as dying and behold they live.

"George R. I., November 11, 1920."

The body was awarded a field marshal's funeral and entombed in Westminster Abbey.

On November 4, 1921, in Rome, the myriad of church and cathedral bells rang out, and a heavy stone slab was closed over the unknown Soldier of Italy buried in the national monument to Victor Emanuel.

The proposal for a similar American ceremony was introduced in Congress just a little more than a month after the French and English rites. Representative Hamilton Fish, Jr., of New York, a veteran of the war, proposed that an unidentified American soldier be returned from France and be buried with full honors in Arlington. Signing the special legislation was one of Woodrow Wilson's last official acts as President of the United States.

In the months following World War I, the armed services went through the grim task of trying to identify their dead. Pathologists in Graves Registration used every device that science had then developed. Bits of uniforms were put under a fluoroscope and all metallic objects—identification tags, rings, watches—were soaked in hydrochloric acid to remove the accumulations of rust in an attempt to read whatever markings there were that might be traceable. Laundry marks were checked. If there were any letters on the body, the handwriting was carefully examined and checked against Army personnel records for a possible clue to the identity of the dead man. Teeth fillings, bone fragments, even skin tissue, were all examined. Only after every test had been applied without success could the Graves Registration Section sign an affidavit that a particular set of remains could not be identified. Finally, 1,647 such affidavits were signed. (In World War II there were 8,494.*)

Most of the American unknowns were buried in four separate military cemeteries in France: Aisne-Marne, Meuse-Argonne, Somme and Saint-Mihiel. On October 22, 1921, a body was taken from each of these four cemeteries** and transported under an honor guard to the city hall of Châlons-sur-Marne for final selection. What little information there was about the bodies, such as the name of the cemetery or the location of the grave site, was destroyed. That night members

* The military makes the distinction between a body that is "unknown" and one that is "nonrecoverable." An "unknown" means that although the body had been recovered it cannot be identified. A "nonrecoverable" occurs when a man is known to be killed but whose body cannot be located, as in an air crash or a ship sunk at sea, or when a man is "missing and presumed dead" but never actually found. There were 3,350 such "nonrecoverables" in World War I and 78,917 in World War II.

** An alternate body was also taken from each cemetery just in case there was some eleventh-hour identification of one of the first four. The precaution proved to be unnecessary and the four alternates were sent back.

of the honor guard shifted the four coffins so that in the morning even the members of the Graves Registration detail could not tell which was which.

At 10 A.M., October 24, 1922, Sergeant Edward Younger, of Chicago, a twice-wounded veteran of the war, reported for special duty outside the venerable city office of Châlons. From somewhere near the city square the muted trumpets of a French military band were playing Chopin. The city was decked in banners and bunting. The flags were at half-staff. Blinking through the sunlight, Younger could make out one big streamer over the main entrance to City Hall, on which was lettered, "Glory to all the heroes unknown."

There were no speeches and little ceremony. An officer handed Younger a spray of white roses and told him, "Place these flowers on any one of them you feel to be your choice. Take all the time you need."

Younger took the flowers and went inside.

"I passed the first one," he said later, "and then the second. Then something made me stop. And a voice seemed to say, 'This is a pal of yours.' I don't know how long I stood there. But finally I put the roses on the second casket and went back into the sunlight."

Eight American noncommissioned officers stepped forward. They lifted the flag-covered coffin and carried it to a waiting chamber and placed it in a metal casket covered with black cloth and decked with silver. Made especially in the United States, the casket bore on its top the inscription, "An unknown soldier who gave his life in the Great War." The other three bodies were taken back for interment in the Meuse-Argonne.

An honor guard, half of American and half of French soldiers, stood watch over the unknown soldier lying at rest

in the rotunda of the City Hall of Châlons-sur-Marne, unadorned except for a spray of white roses that were already
beginning to wilt. This bouquet was never to leave the
soldier and is buried with him.

Until then, 42,453 American dead had been brought home
at the request of the surviving families. Then one man began
a journey home as the symbol of all the lost sons of the war.

The body made its pilgrimage from Châlons by way of
Paris and Rouen to Le Havre, where Admiral Dewey's old
flagship from the Spanish-American War, the *Olympia,* was
waiting. The children of Le Havre fell in behind the gun
carriage and followed it through the streets to the dockside. A
curious harmony was heard that day in Le Havre: first the
muffled drums and trumpet calls of the French Army band
marching ahead, and then the pealing bells of the churches as
the unknown doughboy was brought by.

At pier d'Escale the French paid their last respects. M.
Maginot, the official representative of the French Government, pinned the Legion of Honor on the flag covering the
casket and spoke briefly:

"We do not know thy name; we do not know the name of
thy comrade who lies in Paris under the Arc de Triomphe,
but our gratitude goes out to thee as it does to him. Comrade
from America, though they are about to take thee back to
thine own country, these many French families will always
keep holy thy memory, and we shall ever remember piously
that it was this land of France to which was consecrated thy
last dream."

Then the unknown was lifted aboard the *Olympia.* Under
the shadow of giant guns that twenty-three years before had
fired the opening salvos in the Battle of Manila Bay, the
Navy took over from the Army. A line of eight pallbearers—

six sailors and two Marines—stepped up to the eight soldiers holding the casket. One by one the soldiers stepped away and the sailors and marines took their places. The transfer was made without ever lowering the coffin to the deck.

The unknown was finally placed on a lower deck under a tented awning lined with American flags. Bluejackets, each of them a combat veteran of the war, in shifts of four each, guarded the unknown throughout the fifteen-day voyage home.

Throughout the journey, the *Olympia* displayed both the American and French colors at half-staff. She and her gallant cargo received full salutes and honors from every steamship and sailing vessel encountered on the high seas.

The *Olympia* nosed into the Potomac River on November 9, 1922. The day was foggy and dark with a numbing, slanting rain obscuring the visibility. General John J. Pershing, leading the reception committee waiting at the old Washington Navy Yard, could not see the *Olympia* plowing upstream. But he could hear the heavy thud of artillery as each cannon from military installations along the Potomac boomed a salute to the *Olympia* and her passenger.

At the Yard, a regiment of cavalry waited at attention to receive the coffin. Only an occasional impatient hoof clacking on the wet cobblestones broke the silence.

Then as the *Olympia* made fast, bugles blared out. The pallbearers gently lifted the draped coffin and shouldered it down the gangway. As the body was passed over the side, the shriek of the bos'n's pipe cut the air as the crew of the *Olympia* gave its last farewell to their most honored shipmate.

The coffin was handed to the Army honor guards. A bugle sounded the four flourishes usually reserved for generals. The band struck up the "Star Spangled Banner." The unknown soldier had come home.

The chords of "Onward Christian Soldiers" crashed out and the solemnest of processions clattered over the darkened streets to the Capitol building where the unknown was to lie in state in the rotunda upon the catafalque that first bore the body of Abraham Lincoln.

The President and Mrs. Harding waited in the Capitol rotunda. Mrs. Harding took a broad white ribbon and laid it across the flag-draped coffin still soaked with rain. Next, the President pinned on the official Seal of the United States—a silver shield with forty-eight gold stars.

Then Vice-President Calvin Coolidge, and Chief Justice of the Supreme Court and former President Taft presented their wreaths, followed by other state dignitaries. Finally "Black Jack" Pershing, his straight back unused to bending for anyone, knelt and presented a huge wreath of pink chrysanthemums in the name of the American Expeditionary Force. He stood, drew back, saluted and marched from the room. An honor guard stepped to their places and kept their patient vigil through the dark night.

On November 10, the day before Armistice Day, the unknown soldier lay in state and received the homage of more than 95,000 mourners.

They started to gather around the Capitol long before dawn. At 8 A.M. the doors were opened and the public, four abreast, streamed in. A male chorus sang the verses of "America."

"They sang with a peal of victory and no hint of sorrow," said one reporter who was there.*

---

* Kirke Simpson of the Associated Press, who won a Pulitzer Prize for his coverage of the ceremonies surrounding the entombment of the unknown soldier.

It seemed as if everyone had brought flowers. School children brought flowers from their families' gardens. The British delegation, headed by former Prime Minister Arthur J. Balfour, brought two truckloads of wreaths made from living plants brought from British lands. Sgt. Edward Richardson, of Canada, the oldest living man to wear the Victoria Cross, brought a wreath plaited of poppies from Flanders Field. French Premier Briand brought chrysanthemums. As the blooms piled higher and higher the guards took them away to another chamber, leaving only Mrs. Harding's white sash, the state shield and the withered spray of French white roses that Sergeant Younger had placed at Châlons-sur-Marne. Then the room would fill with blossoms again and again. It was almost midnight when the guards were finally forced to close the doors as still more waited their turn to pay honor to the silent doughboy.

Armistice Day was cold, but the sun had broken through the lowering clouds and the morning was crisp and bright. At 8:02 a single bugle split the air with "Attention." Sabers and rifles snapped to present arms and the coffin carrying the nation's premier hero began its last journey.

From Fort Myer, cannon took up the call and roared a salute. Except when all of America paused for two minutes of silent prayer, the guns at Fort Myer thudded out a salute every sixty seconds until the solemn ceremony was concluded later that afternoon.

Eight World War I veterans, all of whom wore the Congressional Medal of Honor, were the body bearers for the unknown soldier. They were Sergeant Samuel Woodfill, whom Pershing called the greatest American hero of World War I; First Sergeant Harry Taylor of the Army Cavalry; Chief Water Tender Charles O'Connor of the Navy; Sergeant Thomas Saunders of the Army Engineers; First Sergeant Louis Raza of the Army Coast Artillery; Chief Torpedoman James Delaney of the Navy; Staff Sergeant James Dell of the Army Artillery; and Gunnery Sergeant Ernest Janson of the Marine Corps.

These men lifted the coffin onto the caisson drawn by six matched horses and the march to Arlington began.

First came Major General Ernest Bandholtz, commander of the Military District of Washington and grand marshal of the parade. Originally, General Pershing was to have been the grand marshal, but the old AEF commander decided instead to walk behind the caisson bearing one of his fallen troopers.

Behind Bandholtz came an Army band playing a funeral dirge and leading a composite of troops from all the services. A delegation of clergy walked directly ahead of the casket.

The unknown soldier was given a double guard—the row of hero body-bearers walking on either side of the coffin flanked in turn by a row of honorary pallbearers, all generals and admirals. President Harding and General Pershing walked almost alone as the Nation's two chief mourners.

Then came almost every high ranking official and representative of the nation. The Supreme Court marched in a single line. The cabinet officials marched five abreast. Governors, senators and congressmen came next. Those who were veterans wore their uniforms. The lines of congressional gray and khaki were broken by a splash of starched white as Miss Alice Robertson, representative from Oklahoma, marched proudly in her Red Cross uniform.

Veterans from every state in the Union, led by surviving members of the Grand Army of the Republic, marched behind. No foreign decorations were worn that day. Only those granted by America were seen. Although Pershing had ordered that troops should wear all of their American decorations, the old general violated his own order. Walking behind the caisson, he wore only the Victory Medal, which could be worn by every officer and man of the AEF.

At the end of the parade were former President and Mrs. Woodrow Wilson. A dying man, Wilson was making his first public appearance since March 4 when he had accompanied Harding to his inauguration. Wilson was supposed to have ridden in a place of greater honor in the parade but his carriage was held up and he arrived too late to do anything but take a place in the rear.

Traditionally, the route between the White House and the Capitol along Pennsylvania Avenue is one of triumph. Processions normally move up Pennsylvania Avenue to the Capitol when Presidents go to accept their high office or when one of the nation's heroes goes to address a waiting Congress. On that day, however, the solemnest parade Washington had ever seen headed down the Avenue toward Arlington to the steady beat of the "Marche Funèbre."

At the White House, the procession paused for a moment while President Harding and the older members of the official party fell out of the line of march to get into vehicles to drive the rest of the way to Arlington. Pershing, however, kept his place and marched on behind the gun carriage all the way to Arlington.

President Wilson, who had never recovered from the cerebral thrombosis that struck him down the year before while battling unsuccessfully for his beloved League of Nations, was too weak to go to Arlington at all. As he was driven past the White House he tipped his hat to Harding and went home to his family house at 2340 S Street. A group of well-wishers gathered around Wilson's house to cheer him as he went inside. They stayed outside hoping for a word from the commander in chief of the Great War. The former President stepped briefly out into the doorway and waved. He started to say something but no words came out. He stopped for a moment and looked around. His mouth worked a few more times but still there was no sound. Tears came to his eyes. Wilson turned and went inside, never to appear in public again.

The band was pulled out of the line of march. The unknown soldier was taken the rest of the way accompanied only by the sound of marching boots, the beat of muffled drums and the distant thud of cannon from Fort Myer.

The procession was met at the cemetery gate by a Marine band, which led the unknown soldier to the Memorial Amphitheatre.

While Washington moved toward these final services, there erupted an unpredicted comic opera hitch that threatened to make a shambles of the whole ceremony.

The highway bridge leading to Arlington had not been entirely closed to oncoming traffic and one lane was still open. A small touring car coming over the bridge to Washington ran out of gas, and cars behind it tried to pull around, jamming up the stream of traffic heading to the ceremony in Arlington. Within minutes there was the greatest traffic jam in Washington's history—a city with a history of monumental tie-ups.

The President's car was held up five times and the Secret Service men became frenzied while his car bumped hubcaps with jammed automobiles. Once across the bridge his chauffeur repeatedly had to cut off the road over the grass to make headway. Secretary of State Hughes gave up hope of ever crossing the bridge in his official car and walked across. Many dignitaries and bemedaled generals never did make it to Arlington. French Premier Briand was turned away by a guard who thought he was trying to crash the ceremony, and it was only at the last second that the chief delegate from France was able to get to his seat in time for the services.

Briand was also the chief delegate to the Disarmament Conference which was to meet in Washington the next day in the first international attempt to scrap the weapons of global war that were responsible for this day's sad ceremony. To many, the burial services for the unknown soldier were to be more than the final act of piety to the honored dead. They were to be the beginning of bringing truth to the idea that the Great War was indeed the "war to end wars."

The Reverend John Axton sounded the first note in his invocation:

Almighty God, our Gracious Father, in simple faith and trust we seek thy blessing. Help us fittingly to honor our unknown soldiers who gave their all on laying sure foundations of international commonwealth. Help us to keep clear the obligation we have toward all worthy soldiers living and dead that their sacrifices and their valor fade not from our memory. . . .

Facing the events of the morrow, when from the workbench of the world will be taken an unusual task, we ask that Thou wilt accord exceptional judgement, foresight and tactfulness of approach to those who seek to bring about a better understanding among men and nations, to end that discord which provokes war.

As the chaplain finished, the bells of Washington were ringing out the noonday signal. The congregation stood, and for two minutes the entire nation paused and prayed silently. Then a choir sounded the opening chords of "America." The guns of Fort Myer again picked up their doleful sounding and the nation returned once more to normal àctivity.

President Harding was a long way from the ineptitude which marked his administration, when he stood for a moment in front of the crowd at the amphitheatre to pay a nation's last respects to a fallen hero. He spoke slowly so that his words could be picked up by the specially prepared telephone lines that powered his remarks to Chicago, New York and San Francisco. His words reflected the sentiment of the whole nation: prideful of our accomplishments in the war because of what we had already done, hopeful of the future because of what we could do, and futile because of what we had failed to do.

We are met today to pay the impersonal tribute. The name of him whose body lies before us took flight with his imperishable soul. We know not whence he came, but only that his death marks him with the everlasting glory of an American dying for his country.

He might have come from any one of the millions of American homes. Some mother gave him in her love and tenderness, and with him her most cherished hopes. Hundreds of mothers are wondering today, finding a touch of solace in the possibility that the nation bows in grief over the body of one she bore to live and die, if need be, for the Republic. If we give rein to fancy, a score of sympathetic chords are touched, for in this body there once glowed the soul of an American, with the aspirations and ambitions of a citizen who cherished life and its opportunities. He may have been a native or an adopted son; that matters little, because they glorified the same loyalty, they sacrificed alike.

We do not know his station in life, because from every station came the patriotic response of the five millions. I recall the days of creating armies, and the departing of caravels which braved the murderous seas to reach the battle lines for maintained nationality and preserved civilization. The service flag marks mansion and cottage alike, and riches were common to all homes in the consciousness of service to country.

We do not know the eminence of his birth, but we do know the glory of his death. He died for his country, and greater devotion hath no man than this. He died unquestioning, uncomplaining, with faith in his heart and hope on his lips, that his country should triumph and its civilization survive. As a typical soldier of this representative democracy, he fought and died, believing in the indisputable justice of his country's cause. Conscious of the world's upheaval, appraising the magnitude of war the like of which had never horrified humanity before, perhaps he believed his to be a service destined to change the tide of human affairs.

In the death gloom of gas, the bursting of shells and rain of bullets, men face more intimately the great God over all, their souls are aflame, and consciousness expands and hearts are searched. With the din of battle, the glow of conflict, and the supreme trial of courage, come involuntarily the hurried appraisal of life and the contemplation of death's great mystery. On the threshhold of eternity many a soldier, I can well believe, wondered how his ebbing blood would color the stream of human life, flowing on after his sacrifice. His patriotism was none less if he craved more than triumph of country; rather it was greater if he hoped for a victory of all human kind. Indeed, I revere that citizen whose confidence in the righteousness of his country inspired belief that its triumph is the victory of humanity.

This American soldier went forth to battle with no hatred for any people in the world, but hating war and hating the purpose of every war for conquest. He cherished our national rights, and abhorred the threat of armed domination; and in the maelstrom of destruction and suffering and death he fired his shot for liberation of the captive conscience of the world. In advancing toward his objective was somewhere a thought of a world awakened; and we are here to testify undying gratitude and reverence for that thought of a wider freedom.

On such an occasion as this, amid such a scene, our thoughts alternate between defenders living and defenders dead. A grateful Republic will be worthy of them both. Our part is to atone for the losses of heroic dead by making a better Republic for the living.

Sleeping in these hallowed grounds are thousands of Americans who have given their blood for the baptism of freedom and its maintenance, armed exponents of the nation's conscience. It is better and nobler for their deeds. Burial here is rather more than a sign of the Government's favor, it is a suggestion of a tomb in the heart of the nation, sorrowing for its noble dead.

Today's ceremonies proclaim that the hero unknown is not unhonored. We gather him to the nation's breast, within the shadow of the Capitol, of the towering shaft that honors Washington, the great father, and of the exquisite monument to Lincoln, the martyred savior. Here the inspirations of yesterday and the conscience of today forever unite to make the Republic worthy of his death for flag and country.

Ours are lofty resolutions today, as with tribute to the dead we consecrate ourselves to a better order for the living. With all my heart, I wish we might say to the defenders who survive, to mothers who sorrow, to widows and children who mourn, that no such sacrifice shall be asked again. . . .

I speak not as a pacifist fearing war, but as one who loves justice and hates war. I speak as one who believes the highest function of government is to give its citizens the security of peace, the opportunity to achieve and the pursuit of happiness.

The loftiest tribute we can bestow today—the heroically earned tribute—fashioned in deliberate conviction, out of unclouded thought, neither shadowed by remorse nor made vain by fancies, is the commitment of this Republic to an advancement never made before. If American achievement is a cherished pride at home, if our unselfishness among nations is all we wish it to be, and if ours is a helpful example in the world, then let us give of our influence and strength, yea, of our aspirations and convictions, to put mankind on a little higher plane, exulting and exalting, with war's distressing and depressing tragedies barred from the stage of righteous civilization.

There have been a thousand defenses justly and patriotically made; a thousand offenses which reason and righteousness ought to have stayed. Let us beseech all men to join us in seeking the rule under which reason and righteousness shall prevail.

Standing today on hallowed ground, conscious that all America has halted to share the tribute of heart and mind and soul to this fellow American, and knowing that the world is noting this expression of the Republic's mindfulness, it is fitting to say that this sacrifice and that of the millions dead, shall not be in vain. There must be, there shall be, the commanding voice of a conscious civilization against armed warfare.

As we return this poor clay to its mother soil, garlanded by love and covered with decorations that only nations can bestow, I can sense the prayers of our people, of all people, that this Armistice Day shall be the beginning for a new and lasting era of peace on earth, good will among men. . . .

After soprano Rosa Ponselle led a quartet from the Metropolitan Opera House in singing the traditional hymn, "The Supreme Sacrifice," the great of each nation stepped forward to give their highest honors to the unknown soldier.

First, President Harding pinned the Congressional Medal of Honor and the Distinguished Service Cross on the coffin.

Major General Baron Jacques, the representative of Belgium's hero King Albert, stood before the coffin and spoke of his comrade in arms:

We do not know your name, nor your age, nor your birthplace. We know one thing only; you gave your life for us. If we are victorious today, we owe it to your sacrifice, the sacrifice of so many others, the sacrifice which every soldier is ready to make. . . .

I bring to you the last homage we can possibly bestow you.

The general tore the Order of Leopold from his own breast and tenderly laid it on the casket.

Honor fell upon honor. Admiral Beatty, the first sailor of

England, presented the Victoria Cross, which had never before been awarded to anyone but a British subject. Marshal Foch, the Supreme Allied Commander, gave the Légion d'Honneur and the Croix de Guerre. Italian General Armando Diaz brought the Order of the Crown. The highest military honors of Roumania, Poland, Cuba and Czechoslovakia were added.

The dedication ceremonies were ended. Led by the quartet, the mourners sang "Nearer My God To Thee," which had become traditional since the death of President McKinley. The coffin was moved to the narrow crypt on the amphitheatre terrace for the burial service.

Again the soldier was offered up almost as an Old Testament sacrifice to the world's best hope for the next day's Disarmament Conference.

Bishop Brent, formerly the chief chaplain for the AEF, intoned the burial prayer:

Oh God, who, through Thy prophets of old has foretold a day when the armaments of war shall be beaten into the implements of peace, hasten, we beseech Thee, the fulfillment of this, Thy most sure promise. Quell the haughty cries of the nations. Scatter the peoples that delight in wars. Let counsels of peace and unity everywhere prevail, that we may be speedily delivered from our present confusion into the order and righteousness of Thy kingdom.

Before the final commitment there were more honors. Two mothers, one American and one English, put their personal wreaths on the coffin. The American, Mrs. R. Emmet Digney, placed a wreath in honor of all the American mothers who had lost sons to the war. The Englishwoman, Mrs. Julia McCudden, whose son had been shot down in the bitter air war over France, laid a wreath made of red roses grown in England, violets and forget-me-nots from Wales, shamrocks from Ireland, heather from Scotland and white chrysanthemums, maple leaves and lilies from England's overseas dominions.

The first Americans were represented last. American Indian Plenty Coups, chief of the Crow nation, gave the highest tribute of his tribe. He laid his warbonnet and war club among the rest of the honors.

Earth from the battlefields of France had been brought over and spread inside the crypt. The casket was lowered into the crypt and the unknown soldier was again in the soil he had died to help keep free.

Three salvos crashed out of the woods surrounding Arlington, roaring out the signal that the formal ceremony was at an end. Then the sound of taps with its incalculably sweet sadness wished good night and good rest to the fallen soldier. As President Harding led the mourners from the amphitheatre, the cannons sounded again with a 21-gun salute.

The crowd filed out and the unknown soldier was left alone in peace on the slopes of Arlington.

V

BETWEEN WORLD WARS

THE Tomb of the Unknown Soldier was originally a simple stone sarcophagus. Congress had appropriated only $4,000 to put up a subbase for the tomb. The focal point of Arlington was supposed to have been the massive Memorial Amphitheatre nearby. But the tomb symbolic of America's personal sacrifices instead became the place to which everyone came. In 1926 Congress authorized another $50,000 to complete the tomb. The marble, the same that was used in the Lincoln Memorial across the Potomac, was quarried in Colorado and carved to shape in Vermont. Architect Lorimer Rich supervised the completion of the tomb weighing more than 50 tons. It was then that the famous inscription

HERE RESTS IN
HONORED GLORY
AN AMERICAN
SOLDIER
KNOWN BUT TO GOD

was first etched into stone.

The tomb held a fascination for many Americans.

Every day mail and packages poured into Washington.

Some sent flowers, birthday cards, Christmas cards and presents, food, clothes and sometimes just letters.

Despite the most elaborate precautions to guarantee and to publicize that there was not the slightest possibility the body in the tomb could ever be identified, there were still a few mothers and widows from the Great War who clung to the phantom hope.

"My son was 23 years old when he was killed," wrote one woman. "He was blond and had blue eyes. He had a gold tooth in the left upper part of his mouth and wore a St. Christopher's medal around his neck. I know he would never be without it. Does the unknown soldier fit this description?"

"My husband had a birthmark on the palm of his left hand that was shaped like a heart. I never saw anything like it on anyone else. If the unknown soldier has such a mark I know it must be he," wrote another.

To each anguished letter the same answer went out:

"There was nothing, no way, no clue to identify this man. We only know that he was an American."

"Exactly who the men on that hill are is not as important as the fact that they are there," said Arlington Cemetery Supervisor John Metzler.

On the tide of genuine sentiment and national interest, came the lunatic fringe, the unscrupulous and the desecrators.

Until well into the 30's confidence men worked a series of cruel hoaxes on grieving families who had lost sons and husbands in the war. The men would take money from these unsuspecting people by claiming that they could prove that the unknown soldier was actually their kin. Always, the sharpster needed some money to cover his "expenses."

Many people who went to Arlington to visit the cemetery

and see the tomb were shocked to find it desecrated by trash littered about the site and even actual defacement of the tomb itself. Until 1925, guarding the tomb was just another duty of the caretaker of the Memorial Amphitheatre. In November of 1925 a full-time civilian guard was put on duty just to look after the tomb. In March, 1926, the Army decided to watch over its unknown comrade and the first military guard was established. At first the honor guard was on duty only during the daylight hours when the cemetery gates were opened to the public. But, incredibly, vandals would sneak into Arlington at night and desecrate the tomb. In 1937, the guard was ordered to be on duty 24 hours a day and another impressive tradition began out of simple necessity. (See Chapter VIII for the story of the honor guards of the Tomb of the Unknown Soldier.)

With the funeral ceremonies for the unknown soldier in 1922, the American public really believed it was burying the last of its war dead. The "war to end wars" had been won. But less than a year later, an obscure Austrian fanatic named Adolph Hitler jumped up on a table in a beer hall in Munich and fired a revolver into the air.

"The National Revolution has begun," he shouted to the world, and suddenly the world had a new German name to conjure with in their morning newspapers.

On Armistice Day, 1923, still unable to leave his house, Woodrow Wilson spoke over that novelty, the radio, and cried out for a national awakening to the dangers of the world. His hoped-for League of Nations was a shambles; his Versailles Treaty was so much "wastepaper." The glory of the honored dead of World War I now resting in Arlington, Wilson said, was "forever marred and embittered for us by the shameful fact that when the victory was won, chiefly by the indomitable spirit and ungrudging sacrifice of our incomparable soldiers, we turned our backs on our associates; refused to bear any responsible part in the administration of peace or the firm and permanent establishment of the results won by the war at so fearful a cost of life and treasure; and withdrew into a sullen and selfish isolation which is deeply ignoble because [it is] manifestly dishonorable."

The voice of Hitler proved to be stronger than that of Wilson and within 25 years Arlington would again have to open its gates to another flood of war dead.

But all of that seemed very unimportant in the early 1920's as Americans went about the task of heaping honors on their national heroes.

In 1922 the National Geographic Society erected a stone globe with a bronze star at the North Pole in honor of the arctic explorer Robert E. Peary (Section 8) and confirmed the recognition that had almost escaped him for being the first man to reach the North Pole.

The Argonne Cross (Section 18) dedicated to the American dead of World War I still buried in France, was put in place November 13, 1923. That same year Mrs. Harding began what became another charming tradition at Arlington. On behalf of the Girl Scouts of America she planted an elm tree as the first of a series of "living monuments" at Arlington. Two years later the North Carolina Daughters of the Confederacy planted a long-needle pine tree in memory of Anne Carter Lee, the daughter of General Robert E. Lee, who had died at the age of twenty-three in 1862.

At long last the gracious Custis-Lee mansion was cleared of interlopers when in 1925 Congress ordered that the house would no longer be used by cemetery personnel and authorized the funds to restore the house to its original grandeur. In

1933 the mansion and its immediate grounds were separated from the cemetery and turned over to the Department of the Interior to be preserved as a national historical site.

Local historian Enoch Chase was able to report to the Columbia Historical Society in 1931 that "Congress has been fairly generous with funds and the officers of the quartermaster general's office have intelligently applied themselves to the restoration work."

Generous funds and intelligent application notwithstanding, the restoration work was seriously hampered by the fact that many of the heirlooms and their records were lost forever in Mrs. Lee's hasty departure from Arlington Heights. Even as late as the 1930's feelings about the Civil War still ran high. Chase complained that there was little interest from the South in helping to restore the mansion because it was under the control of the North.

Even the placement of the flagpole became a major tempest in a minor teapot. Some old-line Southerners refused to give any antebellum objects to the restoration because they objected to the flagpole flying the stars and stripes in the middle of the view from the stately back veranda. Some historians also objected because there had been no flagpole of any kind when the Lees lived there. The quartermaster general's office at first sided with the historical puritans and attempted to move the pole 100 feet to one side. Veterans of the Grand Army of the Republic however firmly opposed moving the flagpole anywhere. The flag had flown for fifty years over the graves of men who died to preserve the Union,* the GAR said, and it shouldn't be moved. The

* This is a fairly tricky point and depends largely on where you stand. The flagpole is so situated that it can be seen from many of the Union grave sites. However, a person standing at the pole site looking down the steep slope sweeping to the present Memorial Bridge could see almost no Union graves.

quartermaster general found himself in the middle of a violent controversy no matter what he tried to do. Logically, he took the accepted Washington bureaucratic course in the case of controversy. He did nothing and left the pole where it still is today.

On Armistice Day, 1927, a new Cross of Sacrifice was erected to the dead of World War I. This one, the Canadian Cross (Section 46) was dedicated, "by the citizens of Canada in honor of the citizens of the United States who served in the Canadian Army and gave their lives."

The last of the World War I monuments was put into place just before World War II. The Army and Navy Nurses' Memorial was erected in the nurses' section (Section 21) on November 18, 1938, less than a month after Hitler had been given his "last territorial claim" at the appeasement conference in Munich.

Amid the thunderclap of World War II, the changes in Arlington Cemetery were sudden and dramatic. In 1935, when the national shrine was still largely a local cemetery, all of the dead from every war in American history buried in Arlington numbered less than 44,000. By 1949 there were more than 70,000 graves holding the remains of men and women from every state in the Union and 47 foreign nations.*

Group burials, which before had been only for special ceremonies, reflected the mass destruction of World War II and became all too common. Tank and plane crews, officers

---

* Allies who died in America during World Wars I and II were offered sites at Arlington. Many nations brought their dead back for reburial after the war. England, a small country with a history of foreign conflicts, has a long-standing policy to bury her dead where they fall and not return the bodies to their homeland. Axis prisoners of war are also buried in American national cemeteries in keeping with international agreements that prisoners are to be treated with the same basic charities extended to a nation's own soldiers. Sergeant Anton Hilberath, the only German POW in Arlington, is buried in Lot 15, 347-1.

and men, were buried in a single grave as they had perished together in a single machine of war. There are 182 group graves in all of Arlington. The largest of World War II (Section 34) holds the bodies of 250 men who died in World War II off Lunga Beach at Guadalcanal on January 29, 1945, when the USS *Serpens,* a Coast Guard ammunition ship, exploded and sank.

A specially designed Georgia granite obelisk with the name of each man on the *Serpens* was erected by the Government on June 14, 1949.

In 1947 the need for restrictions on land uses became more and more acute. Family burials in the same grave site were authorized. The erection of private monuments and headstones was drastically reduced. In all new Arlington sections, private monuments are now barred and every grave must be marked with a single headstone, which is provided at Government expense. Private monuments are now only allowed in those sections where other private memorials were already in place prior to 1947. Anyone wishing private memorials must clear the design of these structures with the Government, which now demands that they be in harmony with "the spirit of the cemetery today." That means that the stones must be kept fairly simple. Private stones must be maintained at private expense and the Government reserves the right to remove any private memorial not meeting Government standards and replace it with one of the regulation stones. Under no circumstances will the cemetery permit any more of the gingerbread memorials of the turn of the century that charm the historian and appal the modernist. The seemingly indestructible "Black Jack" Pershing died at the age of eighty-eight in 1948. In his will he specified that he wanted no personal monument. His grave (Lot S-19, Section 34), marked by a Government issue headstone, is on a grassy knoll with the men of the old AEF.

The equality of death is present in Arlington. From 1947 on, men were buried without regard to color, creed or rank. Arlington is open to all. In Arizona, the burial ceremony for a hero sergeant was stopped in midservice when authorities were told the sergeant was also a Navajo Indian. His body was brought to Arlington. When civil rights worker Medgar Evers was ambushed and murdered in 1963 his body was brought to Arlington (Section 36–1431). His grave has become a new kind of landmark in Arlington, erected for a man killed in a new kind of struggle.

VI

WORLD WAR II AND THE
KOREAN WAR

O N May 30, 1958, America came again to the Tomb of
the Unknown Soldier, this time bearing two more
sacred bodies—the unidentifiable remains of a fallen warrior
from World War II and one from Korea.

Plans for the entombment of an unknown serviceman from
World War II had been made as early as the summer of 1943
when the Allies began to strike the first hammer blows
against the Axis. On September 10, 1945, four days after
General Douglas MacArthur received the Japanese surrender
on the deck of the USS *Missouri*, legislation was introduced
in Congress to select another unknown dead for the nation's
holiest shrine. The original plan was to entomb the World
War II hero on Memorial Day, 1951. This would have given
the Graves Registration Service time to register, identify or
recover the hundreds of thousands of American dead. On
June 25, 1950, however, elements of the North Korean Army
stormed across the 38th parallel and into South Korea.
America went back to war and formal funeral ceremonies
would have to wait. There would be many more to come.

The idea of making any additions at all to the site of the

Tomb of the Unknown Soldier from the first World War was not entirely popular. Many servicemen felt that the tomb was a perfect memorial to American dead of all wars as it stood. But veterans' organizations, led by the young American veterans of World War II (AMVETS) urged the government to afford this singular honor to the more recent American dead. Under the spur of active veterans' organizations, the Congress acquiesced. The legislation for an unknown dead from World War II was later amended so that an unknown from Korea could also be brought to Arlington.

Selection of the new heroes followed the same general procedure used in choosing the unknown soldier of World War I. But they were greatly expanded to reflect the truly global dimensions that conflict had reached since the "war to end wars" had been fought a quarter of a century before.

There were four separate ceremonies involved in the selection of the unknowns: one to select the unknown from Korea; one to choose an unknown from the Pacific Theatre of World War II, one from the European Theatre of World War II, and a final decision between the two.

The final selection of the Korean unknown took place on the lush, green slopes of Hawaii, where all of the unknown dead of the Korean War are buried. The remains of four unknowns were exhumed and replaced in identically flag-draped caskets. The morning of May 15, 1958, was bathed in the same bright sunlight that had watched over the selection of the unknown soldier of World War I. Master Sergeant Ned Lyle, the Distinguished Service Cross he had won for gallantry in the Korean conflict sparkling in the warm sun, took a wreath of blue and white carnations symbolizing the Korean Service Ribbon and stood at attention in front of the four caskets. He marched briskly to the one on the far left and placed the wreath on it, saluted and turned away.

It may be foolish to compare one ultimate sacrifice with another, but the brief, unemotional ceremony for the unknown soldier from Korea was perhaps the most tragic of all the funeral rites in our history. American men had died to preserve the Union in the Civil War; in a "war to end wars" in World War I; to keep the world free from tyranny in World War II. But here was a man destroyed without even his name to be remembered by, in a fight described by one veteran as "a war we can't win, we can't lose, and we can't get out of."

It was not part of the scheduled services, but following the official ceremony, individual servicemen approached the honored casket and stood at attention for a moment. Each soldier saluted and walked away.

It was determined that the selection of the unknown from World War II would represent the men who fought on all fronts of the most gigantic conflict in our history. Unknown dead were brought to Hickam Air Force Base in Honolulu from both the National Memorial Cemetery of the Pacific in Hawaii and the Fort McKinley American Cemetery in the Philippines. Under an overcast sky Colonel Glenn Eagleston, a combat veteran of both World War II and Korea, approached six caskets with a lei of white carnations to select the Unknown Serviceman from the Pacific. Meanwhile in Europe, Major General Edward O'Neill, United States Army, chose one of 13 unidentifiable dead brought to the Épinal American Cemetery and Memorial in France as the unknown candidate from the European Theatre.

All three bodies were dispatched in solemn ceremony to a rendezvous unique in history. The unknowns from Korea and the Pacific Theatre were flown to the United States Navy base at Guantanamo Bay, Cuba, and transferred to the USS *Boston,* the world's first combat guided missile vessel. The unknown from Europe was brought to Naples and transferred to the waiting USS *Blandy,* one of the nation's newest destroyers. With the crews of both ships maintaining a continuous guard over the unknowns, the *Blandy* and the *Boston* steamed across the Atlantic to meet with America's largest combat vessel in commission, the missile cruiser, USS *Canberra,* where the final selection of the unknown soldier from World War II was to be made.

Sailors in their starched whites stood in a pelting rain as the three ships met in the dark waters that had once been a hunting ground for Nazi U-boats. The unknown from Europe was lifted off the *Blandy* and highlined across to the cruiser *Boston.* The *Boston* and her sister ship, the *Canberra,* then plowed through the roughening seas at ten knots and rigged a line between themselves. One by one, the three unknown dead were pulled across to the *Canberra.* As each one reached the halfway point on the 100-foot highline, a single bugle sounded and the crew of the *Canberra* rendered hand salutes, holding them until the unknown was safely aboard. With the transfer completed, the *Boston* crashed out a salute and steamed off.

The final selection of an unknown serviceman from World War II took place at the stroke of noon on the deck of the *Canberra.* Hospitalman First Class William Charette, the Navy's only holder of the Congressional Medal of Honor on active service, made the final selection by placing a wreath of red and white carnations on one of the caskets. Charette saluted. A choral group sounded the strains of the traditional Navy hymn:

Eternal Father strong to save,
Whose arm doth bind the mighty wave.
Who bidst the mighty ocean deep
Its own appointed limits keep.
Oh hear us when we call to Thee
For those in peril on the sea.

The unknown selected for the final honors at Arlington
was removed, made ready for his final journey, and brought
back aboard the *Blandy* for final transport up the Potomac to
Washington, along with the unknown from Korea. The *Canberra* headed out for deep water to perform its last ceremonial task in honor of the second unknown from World
War II. At two o'clock, the shrill whistle of the bos'n's pipe
screeched and the order "Bury the Dead" was passed over the
loudspeaker. The *Canberra* shut down its engines to full stop
and bobbed quietly in the Atlantic. While the ship's ensign
was dipped to half-mast, a military band played a dirge and
the crew massed on the deck. The remains of the unknown
were taken from his casket and wrapped in the traditional
white sailcloth shroud that serves as the sailor's winding
sheet. Six body-bearers carried the remains to a small mahogany platform in a lower compartment on the starboard
side of the ship. On the order "commit" the bearers tilted the
sliding board, and the weighted canvas shroud slid into the
choppy waves and the body of an unknown hero settled into
113 feet of water.

The *Blandy* moved up the Potomac on the morning of
May 27, her crew standing at attention at the rail, bearing
the two symbols of the ultimate sacrifice of a nation in the
struggle for freedom. The men were borne up the same tragic
route followed by the unknown soldier of World War I to
the rotunda in the Capitol, where they would rest in state on

Entrance to Arlington Cemetery, looking toward the Custis-Lee mansion

The home of Robert E. Lee, also known as Arlington House, as it looked in 1834

Arlington House occupied by Federal troops in 1864

Jacqueline Kennedy, Robert F. Kennedy, Mrs. Rose Kennedy (the President's mother), and other mourners at the funeral of John F. Kennedy

The funeral procession of John F. Kennedy in Arlington

The grave of Private William Christman of Company G, 67th Pennsylvania Infantry, the first Civil War soldier to be buried in the newly created cemetery at Arlington

The Confederate Memorial dedicated by the Daughters of the Confederacy to their Civil War dead

Monument to unknown soldiers who died at Bull Run and on the road to Rappahannock

BENEATH THIS STONE
REPOSE THE BONES OF TWO THOUSAND ONE HUNDRED AND ELEVEN UNKNOWN SOLDIERS
GATHERED AFTER THE WAR
FROM THE FIELDS OF BULL RUN, AND THE ROUTE TO THE RAPPAHANNOCK
THEIR REMAINS COULD NOT BE IDENTIFIED, BUT THEIR NAMES AND DEATHS ARE
RECORDED IN THE ARCHIVES OF THEIR COUNTRY; AND ITS GRATEFUL CITIZENS
HONOR THEM AS OF THEIR NOBLE ARMY OF MARTYRS MAY THEY REST IN PEACE!
SEPTEMBER A. D. 1866.

The mast of the battleship *Maine,* with the Tomb of the Unknown Soldier in the background to the left

The *Maine*'s anchor

Monument to Rear Admiral Robert Edwin Peary, who discovered the North Pole in 1909

The Rotunda at the Tomb of the Unknown Soldier

The Honor Guard at the Tomb of the Unknown Soldier

A horse-drawn caisson at an Army military funeral leaving the chapel at Fort Myer, beside Arlington

U. S. ARMY PHOTOGRAPH

"Blackjack," the caparisoned horse used in military funerals at Arlington

U. S. ARMY PHOTOGRAPH

A member of the United States Army Band plays "Taps" during a funeral ceremony at Arlington

U. S. ARMY PHOTOGRAPH

Model of John F. Kennedy's grave, as seen from the Custis-Lee mansion with the city of Washington in the background

Sketch of John F. Kennedy's grave, looking up the hill toward the Custis-Lee mansion

the sacred catafalque* that had held the bodies of some of the greatest heroes in the history of the Republic.**

The final ceremonies took place on Memorial Day, 1958, and were similar to the rituals surrounding the entombment of the first unknown soldier. The horse-drawn caisson, the marching body-bearers and the muffled drumbeats could have been from the same solemn cortège that had proceeded up Pennsylvania Avenue from the Capitol thirty-seven years before. But the march of time had created new rituals. The traditional military salutes were joined by new ones. Roaring overhead came fifteen Air Force F-100 jet fighters and five medium bombers flying at 1,500 feet in V formations. Each of the V's flew without a right wingman, as a symbol of a missing comrade.

At Arlington, the ceremonies were brief. President Eisenhower spoke only twenty-six words. Rising after the singing of "America the Beautiful," the former supreme allied commander in Europe said, "On behalf of a grateful people, I now present Medals of Honor to these two unknowns who gave their lives for the United States of America."

The two caskets were left above crypts surrounded by floral tributes. Shortly before nightfall, with only a few persons still at hand, the two caskets were lowered into their graves. During the actual ceremonies, the honor guard stopped his regular watch over the tomb for the first time since the creation of the guard. Then a guard stepped forward and the vigil began again.

* The fact that the remains of two heroes would lie in state simultaneously in the Capitol created an unprecedented problem. Only one catafalque had ever been used before. The Lincoln catafalque was duplicated in every detail so that the ceremonies for the two unknowns could be carried out in accordance with established traditions.

** For a complete list of those who have lain in state in the Capitol see Appendix C.

VII

THE MILITARY FUNERAL

NOT since the ceremonies surrounding the entombment of the unknown soldier of World War I has Arlington witnessed anything to match the pageantry of the state military funeral accorded to Lieutenant John F. Kennedy, USNR, 35th President of the United States, struck down on November 22, 1963.

The state funeral is given only to Presidents or to those whom the President may designate. But the basic formula for the military funeral at Arlington remains the same for everyone—President, general or private.

In all cases, the traditions of the American military funeral stretch back into the centuries to steal from the burial service its sadness and transform it into one of glory and pride of service and country.

In most cases the known origins of the rituals of the military funeral are lost. The majority of them appear to have originated as battlefield expedients for meeting what has always been the sacred obligation of soldiers to bury their dead.

The tradition of the caparisoned, or hooded, horse such as

the seventeen-year-old gelding "Blackjack" who followed behind President Kennedy's caisson, goes back to the campaigns of Genghis Khan. His Mongol warriors believed the spirit of a cavalryman's horse would accompany the fallen warrior and serve him again in the next world as it had in this one.

Gradually the custom grew of sacrificing a horse at a soldier's funeral. In Europe it was commonly believed that if a horse was not sacrificed it could not find its master after death and the warrior's spirit would have to walk.

When American Plains Indians began to use horses, they adopted the burial custom of the white man. Blackbird, a great chief of the Omahas was buried sitting on his favorite war-horse.

Boots reversed in the stirrups and the sword thrust through the saddle blanket are a custom of the feudal wars and signify that the fallen soldier will never ride again in life. At Fort Myer special saddles with boots and sword permanently fixed in place are kept ready for military funerals. Traditionally, the ritual of the riderless horse is performed only for generals of any Army branch or a commissioned officer who served in a mounted unit during his career. Presidents and those designated by the President may also be accorded this honor.

The custom of transporting the body on a gun carriage or caisson was undoubtedly a battlefield expedient and can be traced back to the days of Henry VIII in England.

Many of the traditions of the military funeral reverse the normal order of things to signify the great reversal of life by death. The flying of the flag at half-staff was originally done to signify the physical victory of death over life. Traditionally, honorary pallbearers accompanying the cortège march to the mournful quickstep in reverse order of their ranks with the lowest ranking officer leading the group.

The 21-gun salute accorded President Kennedy was another custom stemming from the most ancient of military ceremonies. The concept of the gun salute stems from the days of wooden sailing ships. In the days of slow-firing guns when it took a long time to load and rearm between salvos, the ship that spent its shot in ceremonious salute showed it placed itself completely within the power of the other vessel and was at its disposal. When Britannia really ruled the waves, English vessels liked to force the ships of other nations to fire the first salute. Eventually, however, international usage developed the "gun-for-gun" principle of equality for all nations, and each ship fired salutes together.

The figure of 21 guns as the highest national honor started as a British concept going back to 1875. The British national salute was seven guns for a ship. Because gunpowder of sodium nitrate could be more easily stored on land than at sea, shore batteries so powered were allowed three shots for each one of a ship's. When powder was improved by using potassium nitrate, ships of the line improved their gunnery potential and were able to match the salute of shore batteries. Prior to 1875 there was considerable confusion on the international scene as to how many guns one country or ship should allot to another. John Paul Jones set the precedent for the United States when his ship, while sailing in Quiberon Bay off France, received the first salute ever given to an American vessel. Jones replied with a 13-gun salute, one for each state. As the number of the states increased so did the number of American gun salutes. Social problems on the high seas also mushroomed as the ships of monarchies began to insist on receiving more guns than they gave to those of republics. Finally in 1875 the United States and Britain, as the two major seapowers of the world, formally agreed on 21 guns as the highest international salute. The practice became generally accepted among all nations.

Traditions of the loftiest sentiment can have the meanest beginnings. At President Kennedy's tragic funeral, the chill November air was rent from time to time with the flourishing sounds of "Hail to the Chief." This music, now played officially only for Presidents, was for more than thirty years a popular tune for music hall tenors during the early part of the nineteenth century. In 1810 James Sanderson, an English popular songwriter was commissioned to set portions of Sir Walter Scott's classic poem, "The Lady of the Lake" to music for a dramatic presentation. The hit of the production was Sanderson's tune for the Boat Song:

> Hail to the Chief, who in triumph advances!
> Honoured and blessed be the ever-green Pine!
> Long may the tree in his banner that glances,
> Flourish the shelter and grace of our line!

The song was heard in America by 1811 and until well into the 1840's the tune with a myriad of plagiarized lyrics and parodies became a musical staple.

Because of its popularity and stirring martial air, "Hail to the Chief" was a natural to be used in political rallies whenever the candidate appeared. Eventually—no one knows exactly when—it began to be played at Presidential inauguration ceremonies. Over the years, the air became more and more associated with the office of the President and is now reserved only for the man who holds that office.

The crackling volley of three shots over the grave is another ceremony of ancient lineage. Opposing armies, their weapons in reverse, would pause from the carnage of battle and allow a truce for each side to dispose of the fallen. The three shots signified that burial ceremonies were over and the army was prepared to do battle again.

The use of the American flag as a coffin drape stems from another battlefield expedient. Flags were often used as temporary shrouds to protect the dead in combat zones until coffins could be constructed or the body buried in a field grave. Today, the flag symbolizes that the deceased served his country in the military.

The tradition under which Mrs. Kennedy received the flag that covered her husband's casket, however, is of more recent origin. In 1903, George Cocheu, a second lieutenant fresh from West Point, was in an honor guard at Fort Sheridan, Illinois, to receive the body of an officer who had died while on duty in the Philippines. Lieutenant Cocheu was shocked to find that the flag which had covered the coffin all the way from the Pacific was taken away at the railroad station and the officer's grieving family received only a drab wooden box for final burial. Cocheu was told that the Army had strict regulations on the accountability of equipment, and that the quartermaster had to take back the flag or declare it lost and try to make someone pay for it.

The memory of the bare coffin rankled for years, until Cocheu was assigned as a major to the War Department in 1918. He requested permission to draw up new procedures for military funerals. His recommendations were incorporated into the service and have become some of the most cherished parts of the ceremony: that a firing squad be provided for each military funeral; that a body be accompanied by a soldier of at least the same rank as the dead man or higher; and that the flag be left on the coffin and eventually given to the next of kin.*

The sound of taps at the end of a burial ceremony, wishing the serviceman "good sleep until the eventual reveille to come," was first heard in the Civil War. Originally, the American Army used the French *"L'Extinction des Feux"* ("Lights Out") as the final bugle of the day. While this call was supposed to have been the favorite of Napoleon, it grated on the tin ear of Union General Daniel Butterfield.

The General was tone-deaf, but he knew what he liked. He set about inventing his own call that sounded better to him for calling an end to the day's activities. Working with the brigade bugler, Oliver Norton, General Butterworth created the haunting three-note refrain one hot July night during a lull in the Peninsular Campaign of 1862.

It was soon adopted by the other corps and later was made official throughout the Army.**

Taps as a funeral call was also first used in the Peninsular Campaign. According to the generally accepted account, a soldier in "A" Battery of the 2nd Artillery was buried at a time when the battery occupied an advance position concealed in the thick woods. It would have been dangerous to sound the customary three rifle volleys, because the battery, hidden in the trees, was too near the southern positions of the enemy, and the firing might have touched off an artillery exchange.

The Battery Captain ordered the bugler to play "Taps" for

* The presentation of the flag must be made by an official representative of the U.S. Government, either military or civilian. It cannot be presented by a civilian clergyman, or any person not connected with the Government.

** In 1932, the French Army dropped its *"L'Extinction des Feux"* in favor of the American "Taps." In the American Army, the "Lights Out" call is still used as "Tattoo," a call sounded at nine at night signifying "repair to quarters."

their dead comrade. The strain cut across the quiet battle-field, and another tradition was born.

Later words were fitted to this simplest and most moving of melodies:

> Fades the light
> And afar
> Goeth day
> Cometh night;
> And a star
> Leadeth all,
> Speedeth all
> To their rest.

VIII

THE HONOR GUARD

THE sentinels on guard at Arlington are members of one of the oldest and most honored of American military units, the historic Third Infantry Regiment. Organized before the Constitution for which it has fought in scores of actions, today it is known as the "Old Guard" or the "President's Own." The honor guard of the Third are a rough equivalent of the household cavalry that has protected the kings and queens of England from early history.

The Third is a sometimes curious amalgam of America's oldest and newest fighting units. While some members of the unit drill to the exact precepts laid down during the Revolution by the first Army drillmaster, Baron von Steuben, the Third still carries as its primary mission the tactical defense of Washington in case of either ground attack or civil disorder. Muskets and M-14's are all part of its standard armory equipment.

Established in 1784, the Third was blooded during the Revolution and has been a part of the American military heritage ever since. It carries several honors not permitted other American units. The Third was the only Army unit allowed to depict the shield of the United States on its coat of arms.

As a result of gallantry during the Mexican War, the Third won yet another laurel. General Winfield Scott, the commander of the American Expeditionary Forces, and as exacting a commander as the United States ever put into the field, watched the courageous Third storm the high ground in the bitterly contested action at the battle of Cerro Gordo in 1847. Not given to superlatives, "Old Fuss and Feathers" noted in his diary:

"The style and execution which I had the pleasure to witness was most brilliant and decisive. The brigade ascended the long and difficult slope without shelter and under tremendous fire of artillery and muskets, with the utmost steadiness, reaching the breastwork; drove the enemy from there, planted the colors with the enemy's flag still flying—and after some sharp firing finished the conquest with the bayonet."

After that, the Third was given special permission to march in review with fixed bayonets.

One President, Zachary Taylor, served in the Third, as well as a score of men who later gained prominence in the military and diplomatic service of the country.

Today the Third, with the unwieldy proper name "1st Battalion (Reinforced) Third Infantry," performs a number of highly specialized ceremonial tasks in addition to its primary mission of the defense of the capital. Members of the 1,100-man Third act as the official military escort for the President when he is in Washington and also participate in the ceremonies granted to foreign dignitaries arriving in America. A special 36-man fife and drum corps was created in 1960 after exhaustive historical research. The group became famous when it played at Mount Vernon during the state visit of President Ayub Khan of Pakistan and marked the first time a President had entertained on the Mount Vernon grounds since George Washington.

Drilling to the specifications laid down by von Steuben in 1779 "for the order and discipline of the troops of the United States" the troops are accurate to the last shoe buckle and oblique march movement. The caisson section, the only United States Army unit which still maintains a stablemaster, saddler and blacksmith on its duty roster, is responsible for the honor funerals at Arlington. Finally, there is the elite honor guard which stands perpetual watch over the Tomb of the Unknowns.

The two units most closely associated with Arlington are the caisson section and the honor guard.

The caisson section runs 3,000 military funerals a year, and has been known to handle as many as 27 in a single day. The section's complement consists of 26 horses, 12 blacks and 14 grays, and 20 men to handle the details of the military funeral. Although the normal duty day does not begin until 7 A.M., most of the men find they have to get to work as early as 5:30 to take care of the barnyard chores of polishing tack, grooming and exercising the horses which take about two and half hours.

In the funeral itself, there are usually three pairs of horses —a lead team, a swing team and a wheel team—to pull the caisson. Each team has a single rider on the left horse, while a fourth man, "the chief of section," rides an unhitched horse and is in charge of the caisson detail during the ceremonies.

Out of the overall Third Infantry troop, there is a selected group of 190 men who form the honor guard. They perform the more exacting of the ceremonial duties performed by the

Third, and are the closest American approximation of the royal guards of the British Crown.

The entrance requirements, both physical and mental, for the honor guard are more stringent than for any other outfit in the Army. On state occasions a guard member must handle himself with the aplomb of an experienced diplomat.

"You never know who is going to stop and talk to one of the men," an officer said, "and when the President of a country asks a question he expects a quick and lucid answer. Our men can think on their feet and have gotten so used to meeting dignitaries from all over the world, nothing seems to faze them any more."

Physically, a member of the guard must be between 5 feet 11 inches and 6 feet 1 inch, with no visible defects or blemishes. His discipline record must also be spotless.

Out of this honor guard the men who stand watch over the unknowns are culled. Even for a member of the honor guard, an additional two to three months of intensive training are required before going on duty in front of the tomb.

The spit and polish is incredible. Boots are polished every few hours during a day's tour of duty. Haircuts are expected every few days. Although a soldier walks his post in front of the tomb for one hour at a time during daylight, he generally puts on a fresh uniform for each swing. The men go over their patches with lighted matches to clear them of any fuzz. Neckties are fastened with adhesive tape. Lint is simply not allowed to exist.

The measured cadence in front of the tomb does not vary. Every hour, the guard walks his post 42 times at exactly 120 paces per minute. The procedure is unrelenting in its exactitude—21 paces in front of the tomb, turn and face the city of Washington for exactly 20 seconds, turn again and face the tomb for 20 seconds, execute the manual of arms and march back to the other end of the rubber mat inside the gold chain and repeat. The guard keeps his rifle on his shoulder away from the tomb and toward the crowd at all times. The routine is varied at night when the tour of duty is two hours instead of one.

The guard is always prepared to break and stop anyone who might be foolish enough to try to enter the tomb area itself. But other than that he remains on his post and leaves the minor problems to the civilian policeman on hand. A few exceptions are made for bad weather. In heavy rain or snow the sentinel may stay in the sentry box at parade rest for a time. But even in stormy weather he must walk his post every ten minutes.

His military bearing must be, and is, unbreakable. Even a casual look at one of the guards shows that none of them is a boy playing at dress-up soldier. The set of the jaw and steadiness of the brow attest to the seriousness of the trust placed in the man.

Above the door of the guards' quarters leading out to the tomb area there is a sign with the imprimatur of the guards. It says simply:

"The World's Best."

IX

ARLINGTON LOOKS TO
THE FUTURE

B Y 1965 a clear picture of Arlington's future was in focus. It was obvious there would be changes in Arlington both in its physical appearance and in its tone. The changes would not seem radical, at first glance. Except for the size of the cemetery itself, and the addition of the Kennedy grave-site, Arlington in 1990 will probably not appear widely different from Arlington in 1965. It will, however, be a far cry from the rustic cemetery of 1890.

Arlington National Cemetery irrevocably altered its course on November 11, 1921, when the Tomb of the Unknown Soldier of World War I was dedicated. From that day on, Arlington ceased to be a pastoral, semiprivate resting ground for the career military, and instead became a national shrine. Its growth and mood were permanently influenced.

Most of what has taken place since then has been, with the exception of the introduction of the Kennedy grave, relatively predictable. Arlington gradually became more of a national shrine and less of a simple cemetery. It also rapidly approached capacity.

Until 1965, Arlington's area was fixed at 420 acres. Then

the expansion into the available adjacent land at Fort Myer began. Congress appropriated money for the first stage of expansion: the development of two plots, some 30 acres in the upper two corners of the fort's south post. This was not really a sudden, unforeseen move. In 1924 the Secretary of War, with the backing of the Capital's Fine Arts Commission, officially announced the Army's intention to expand the cemetery to the Fort Myer area. This plan came close to going by the boards in the late 1930's when Government planners, searching for a site for the Pentagon, cast covetous eyes on the Fort Myer area. Finally another location was chosen for that mammoth structure, and the blueprint for the Arlington expansion was safe. Indeed, it was reaffirmed with an additional provision: no large permanent structures were ever to be built on the south post.

The south post contains some 202 acres. The Army estimates that all of it will be part of the cemetery by 1976. Total cemetery burial space should last until sometime in the late 1980's. (Army planners have found that exact or nearly exact forecasts are impossible because of unforeseen factors.) At this time Arlington will technically become "closed" and the only burials will be in spaces already assigned. The geographical situation of the cemetery makes it virtually impossible for any expansion once the Fort Myer land is used. In fact, the planned expansion runs counter to the Government's policy on national cemeteries, established in 1961, which ruled out any further expansion of existing national cemeteries. Arlington's south post project was the only exception.

The Army term "closing" to describe what will occur in the late 1980's is an official term. It means that all space in Arlington is either occupied or committed, and that there will be no further burials after existing commitments have been carried out. An eligible widow whose husband reserved space for her, or who wishes to share her spouse's grave site, will not be barred from burial in Arlington after the "closing" date.

The eventual acreage of Arlington can be predicted exactly by adding the present 420 acres to the south post's 202 acres. The resulting computation of 622 acres is likely to be the permanent size of the cemetery. Population totals, however, are a different matter. The Army refuses to estimate or even guess at the future population of Arlington. But by utilizing an established rule of thumb of 600 burials per acre, and by observing the national growth rate, it is possible to come up with a rough idea. For example, during the fiscal year ending June 30, 1962, there were 4,578 burials at Arlington. In fiscal 1963 the figure was 4,591. In fiscal 1964 it went up to 5,773. A 6,000-a-year average for the next twenty-four years would produce a final population total in the neighborhood of 270,000. This would be about 144,000 more than the 126,608 persons buried in Arlington National Cemetery as of September 30, 1964.

The current high number of burials is due to many factors. Chiefly, the death rate for World War I veterans is just now reaching its peak. Additionally, more and more veterans of World War II are approaching the insurance company actuarial limits. These are the factors that can be calculated years ahead. In the 1940's the Army foresaw the 1960's as the start of the heavy inflow. Then there are the unforeseen factors. The influence of the burial of President Kennedy in Arlington was one. The popularity of Arlington as a burial ground rose sharply immediately after his funeral on November 25, 1963. During November, 1963, 407 persons were buried in Arlington. In December there were 529. One year later the pace had slackened. But it still maintained a level of 502 a month. The daily average rose from 18 before the Kennedy funeral to 24. The burial of President Kennedy in Arlington accelerated the already increasing rate of growth at Arlington. Whether that extra acceleration will prevail over the years is impossible to tell. If it should last, it would mean that Arlington could close a few years earlier than the "late 1980's" expectation.

While unexpected factors might hasten the closing of Arlington, something could also happen which might put off the cemetery's closing date. On October 16, 1961, for example, the Defense Department announced a new policy for Arlington, under which all members of an eligible family would be buried in a single grave site. The "one grave site" rule, previously observed in many cemeteries in crowded metropolitan areas, could prolong the active use of Arlington for as much as five years. Using some of the existing roadways for burial space would be another way of extending the land use of Arlington. But this would make for a predictably unpopular decision to eliminate, or at least sharply curtail, private automobile traffic throughout Arlington. When all possibilities are taken into account, however, the Army's late 1980's estimate for closing the cemetery seems reasonable.

The future of Arlington must also be considered within the context of the national cemetery system. While Arlington is the most renowned of the country's 85 national cemeteries, it is neither the largest nor the oldest. Many years from now, well beyond the late 1980's closing date of Arlington, it is probable that virtually no one will be buried in any national cemetery. All of them will have been closed, because they will have reached capacity or simply have been shut down because they were infrequently used due to their remoteness. In any event, the national cemetery system will not grow. That was established during 1961, when Congress requested an overall review of the national cemetery policies. The study, written by the administration under heavy pressure from funeral directors and private cemetery interests, concluded that "further expansion of the existing system would be inadvisable." It noted, quite accurately, that the original purpose of the national cemeteries to provide for the burial of soldiers who had died *in service* had been so distorted that by 1961 fewer than ten percent of those buried in national cemeteries were persons who died on active duty, or their families. As of 1961, more than 40 million persons were eligible for burial in national cemeteries—clearly beyond the system's capabilities. The study also said the system discriminated against those who did not happen to live near a national cemetery. The most active cemeteries were those close to large metropolitan areas, but not all metropolitan areas have national cemeteries and expansion of the national cemetery system would just extend that discrimination. In addition, "the enormous cost which would result from furnishing burial facilities for even a fraction of the more than 40 million presently eligible individuals would be prohibitive." Burial benefits provided under the Social Security system and the Veterans' Administration to be utilized in private facilities, the study said, were far preferable to facilities to be furnished by the Government.

The Administration study held that Arlington was a special case and should be exempt from the policy at least to the extent of allowing expansion to the south post of Fort Myer under the 1924 plan. But it made it clear that this would be the only exception.

There is always the possibility that Congress might overturn that policy. But no serious effort has been made since it was enunciated. Since World War II only one cemetery, at Fort Logan, near Denver, Colorado, has been added to the national system.

Most Americans seem to have gone along with this phasing out of the system primarily because many noncareer veterans have never thought seriously about being buried in a military cemetery, in spite of the rising costs of funerals. Counterbalancing the free plot of land offered by the Government are the often considerable transportation costs connected with getting the deceased to the cemetery. There is also the matter of visiting. Family or friends who wish to visit the grave naturally find it difficult to travel a long distance to pay their respects.

Affecting both the physical and spiritual quality of Arlington is the grave of John F. Kennedy. The tomb and its accompanying landscaping features have rivaled the Tomb of the Unknown Soldier as a focus of attention. Far more than a memorial to a man it is the symbol of a vast national tragedy.

The land area itself, rolling away from the Custis-Lee mansion down to the Potomac, is one of the most important pieces of land in the Capital. The French critic Augustus Saint-Gaudens wrote in 1902:

The noble slope toward the river should be rigorously protected against the invasion of monuments which utterly annihilate the sense of beauty and repose. This is one of the most beautiful spots in the vicinity of Washington; it should not be defaced or touched in any way, and a law or rule should at once be passed forbidding the placing of any monument on this hill.

The architect's problem was to create a monument strong enough to befit the enormity of the American calamity and understated enough to do no violence to the beauty of the slope.

The answer has been a four-part design.

The simple grave lies on a grassy slope 280 feet below the Custis-Lee Mansion. Behind the grave is the Eternal Flame, cupped in a triangular bronze font and engineered to remain lit in all weather. Between the flame and the mansion is a long, low wall terminating the site, which also serves to make the site more visible. Called a "vertical backstop" by the *New York Times* architecture critic Ada Louise Huxtable, this feature has been the most controversial of the design. Cut into its stone is the Seal of the President of the United States. The grave site is set on a 42 by 66 foot white marble terrace, which appears to float on the slope.

Below the terrace is a paved, circular walk of granite that leads to an elliptical overlook that will hold about 1,000 people. Serving as a bottom lip to the overlook is a low, tapered wall. On it will be inscribed quotations from President Kennedy's inaugural and other addresses. As the visitor to the grave site reads these words he can look up and see the panorama of Washington that lies below him to the east.

The grave was lined up along the Great Axis of Washington, extending from the Capitol through the Lincoln Memorial and across the Potomac River to the mansion. Engraved on the President's 34 by 52 inch grave marker are a small cross and the words:

John Fitzgerald Kennedy
1917–1963

★ 84 ★

On either side of the grave are two smaller markers for the graves of the Kennedys' two deceased infants, Patrick Bouvier Kennedy and the unnamed "Baby Girl Kennedy."

The grave site plan was conceived by John Carl Warnecke, who worked closely with Mrs. Kennedy and other members of the Kennedy family. It was made public on November 16, 1964. Construction was scheduled to begin in the fall of 1965 and take about one year to complete. The Kennedy family are to pay all costs associated with the grave site itself. The Defense Department asked Congress to appropriate funds for the remaining features, since the grave will be a national monument as well as a private grave. Preliminary estimates put the Kennedy family's share of the expenses between $200,000 and $400,000. The cost to the Government for all the other construction, engineering and landscaping was expected to total about $2 million. Once built, it will be maintained out of the regular Arlington budget.

In spite of its national prominence, the designers of the Kennedy grave were mindful that the President was being laid to rest in a military cemetery. Except for the "backstop" wall the simplicity of Arlington was largely continued in the plan and is probably its most impressive feature. The plain gray slate tablet marking the grave not only symbolizes the New England background of the late President, it is in keeping with the simple grave markers now standard throughout the cemetery.

In designing the grave, Warnecke and his associates also had to create something that would blend with the neighboring Custis-Lee Mansion and still reflect the office of the Presidency without attempting to evaluate the Kennedy record. At the same time it had to be able to accommodate the thousands of ordinary citizens who stop by daily, as well as dignitaries who come to pay their respects in official ceremonies.

In the ensuing years, Arlington will take on more of the trappings of a tourist attraction. While this endangers the inherent solemnity of a cemetery, the particular serenity and dignity of Arlington need not necessarily be sacrificed.

The crush of visitors to the cemetery will grow larger. The number of tourists to Washington in 1980 is expected to be triple what it was in 1964. Because of the Kennedy grave site and the Tomb of the Unknowns, many of these visitors will undoubtedly include a trip to Arlington in their itineraries. During the first summer after the Kennedy assassination an average of 50,000 people a day streamed past the grave.

With this tremendous boost in overall numbers came an inevitable increase in the negative features of tourism: litter, noise, and a general disrespect for the surroundings. But Arlington officials have been philosophical. These unpleasantnesses had been known since the Tomb of the Unknown Soldier of World War I was dedicated in 1921. The added number of visitors prompted by the Kennedy memorial meant only that there would be a few more of these infuriating nuisances. Actually, Arlington fares better than most tourist attractions throughout the country. Many people who might drop paper bags around "Old Faithful" check themselves when they remember they are in a national cemetery. The same cannot be said for the Washington Monument or our national parks. This however, is not a great consolation to grieving families who come to Arlington to bury or honor their dead and find the area overrun with noisy tourists making just another stop-off on their way to see the District of Columbia Armory.

The perseverance with which the Army cares for Arlington is perhaps the best insurance for continued respect by the overwhelming majority of those who visit the cemetery. The upkeep of the landscaping, the maintenance of the grave sites, and the military routine all contribute to an Arlington that it is to be hoped will not materially change in tone.

Arlington National Cemetery can never again be the pastoral, almost exclusive institution that it once was. But it will be something meaningful to many more people if it can continue to be both a beautiful resting place for the dead and a constant reminder of our national heritage, for the living. It will then truly be not for one man, not for one army nor even for one war, but for all time.

Appendices

REGULATIONS ON ELIGIBILITY FOR BURIAL AT ARLINGTON

THE regulations covering the eligibility requirements for persons wishing to be buried at Arlington Cemetery are the same throughout the national cemetery system. Basically, they provide that any member, male or female, of the armed services, who is either on active duty at the time of death or who has been honorably discharged, may be buried at a national cemetery such as Arlington. An adult who is dependent on the service member or the service member's estate, at the time of the dependent's death is also eligible.

The key to eligibility for burial in Arlington or any national cemetery is the condition of the discharge of the service member. For instance, a soldier who was honorably discharged from the service and later became a convict could still be eligible for burial at Arlington, while a man who was discharged under any conditions other than honorable, even though he may have won the Congressional Medal of Honor, would not be eligible.

The following is an analysis of the Government regulations which have been checked by cemetery officials for accuracy. In cases where Arlington is named the same rules apply to all other national cemeteries.

REQUIREMENTS FOR ELIGIBILITY

1. Members and former members of the armed forces

Any member of the armed services who dies while on active duty is eligible. Any citizen who served in the armed services and was honorably discharged is eligible. The term of service does not have to have been during time of war. Any United States citizen who served in an armed service of an ally of the United States during a war in which the United States was a belligerent, is eligible. Here, wartime service is required.

2. Members of reserve components

Membership in a reserve component of the armed services by itself does not make a person eligible for burial in Arlington. However, members of a reserve component of any of the armed services, members of the Army National Guard, Air National Guard, members of the Reserve Officer's Training Corps of the Army, Navy or Air Force, are eligible for burial in a national cemetery if death occurs while serving on active duty for training, or while performing full time service as a reservist or guardsman. Certain members of these organizations who die while hospitalized or undergoing treatment at Government expense for injury or disease contracted or incurred under honorable conditions while on duty or service or traveling to or from duty or service *may* be eligible.

3. Commissioned officers in the Coast and Geodetic Survey

The special regulations concerning officers in the Coast and Geodetic Survey prescribe that a commissioned officer who was released from service with an honorable discharge is eligible for burial in Arlington if in World War II he was assigned to an area listed as one of immediate military hazard, if he was assigned to the Philippine Islands on December 7,

1941, or if he was actually transferred to the Department of the Army or Navy under the provisions of a special act of Congress passed on May 22, 1917.

4. Members of the Public Health Service

Commissioned officers of the Public Health Service qualify for burial in Arlington if they were detailed for duty with the Army or Navy during World War I or served at any time between December 8, 1941, and July 3, 1952.

5. The spouse of an eligible service member

The spouse of an eligible service member may be buried in the same grave in which the service member has been or will be buried if space is available. Widows or widowers of members of the armed services lost, buried at sea, or for some other reason officially declared to be permanently absent, missing or missing in action, may also be buried in a national cemetery of their choice if space is available. A widow or widower who remarries may be buried at Arlington only if her spouse at the time of her death is also eligible.

If the spouse of an eligible service member dies first, he or she may be buried in Arlington only if, prior to burial, the surviving service member signs an agreement to be buried in the same grave.

6. Minor children

The minor children of an eligible service member may be buried in Arlington only in the same grave in which either parent has been or will be buried. If the minor child should die first, the service member must sign the same sort of agreement as stated in the preceeding paragraph.

7. Adult children

The burial of unmarried children over twenty-one years of age is authorized in Arlington only if they are unmarried and physically or mentally disabled and incapable of self-support, and are dependent on the service member or others if both parents are dead. The burial of adult children will be allowed only on prior approval from the Office of the Chief of Support Services in Washington. Requests for permission should be sent to the superintendent of the national cemetery in which burial is desired. Such a request must be accompanied by a notarized statement on the marital status and degree of dependency of the deceased child as well as the name or the service-connected parent. A certificate from the physician who attended the child as to the nature and duration of the physical or mental disability must also be submitted.

Many elderly persons, mostly surviving parents of service members, had been under the misapprehension that they were eligible, and had written to Washington to request that they be buried with the service member. Up until 1948 authorities in Washington made a certain number of exceptions and granted some of these persons advance permission *in writing*. The Government will honor those commitments made up until 1948, but it has not made any more exceptions.

GRAVE SITE RESERVATIONS

Regulations do not allow persons to reserve a specific grave site. Grave sites are assigned only upon immediate requirement for burial.

PROCEDURES FOR REQUESTING BURIAL

At the time of death of a person eligible for burial in Arlington, the mortician or person responsible for making the funeral arrangements should submit a request for burial directly to the cemetery superintendent. The request should furnish such information as the name, rank, serial number, date of death and dates of entry and separation from the last service of the person upon whose military connection the request is being made. Remains should not be shipped nor should final time of burial be set until all arrangements with the superintendent have been completed and he has authorized shipment for burial at a specific time and date. Except in cases where the remains have to be shipped over long distances, these arrangements can be made as quickly as in a regular cemetery.

It is a good idea to keep all pertinent service records, burial data and instructions with your personal papers for use when required.

EXPENSES

There is no charge for the grave site at Arlington or for the opening and closing of the grave itself. Headstones are also provided at no charge. Other burial services and benefits may be provided at Government expense for members of the armed forces who die while on active duty. The services and benefits provided can vary with the circumstances, and information should be obtained from the service to which the member was assigned at the time of death.

The incidental expenses such as preparation, casketing and transportation from the place of death to Arlington for any former member of the armed services must be met out of private funds. There are certain cases in which the Veterans Administration will make a burial allowance available. Inquiry about this should be made to the nearest VA office.

MILITARY CEREMONIES AND HONORS

The rendition of military ceremonies or honors depends on the rank of the deceased (see Chapter Seven on the military funeral) and on the availability of troops at the armed forces installation near the cemetery. If troops are not available, the next of kin may be able to arrange for the rendition of honors by members of local veterans' organizations. Although the cemetery superintendent is not specifically authorized to assume responsibility for providing honors, in most cases he will be able to assist the next of kin if desired. At Arlington the providing of requested honors can always be assured. There is no charge for honors.

PERSONS INELIGIBLE FOR BURIAL

1. Adult relatives such as fathers, mothers and in-laws are not eligible for burial in Arlington by reason of their relationship to a service member, regardless of whether they are members of his household (except where permission has been granted in writing prior to 1948).

2. Discharge other than honorable

Persons whose last separation from the service was under any conditions other than honorable are not eligible regardless of any honors or decorations received and notwithstanding the fact that they might have received veterans' benefits, treatment in a VA hospital or that they died in such a hospital.

3. Conviction of a crime

A person convicted of a crime which results in the loss of United States citizenship, or convicted in a state, federal or military court of a crime for which the *maximum* penalty is death or exceeds fifteen years' imprisonment (regardless of the actual term imposed) may not be buried in Arlington. An exception to this rule is granted if a person, subsequent to such a conviction, should serve in an armed service and either dies while in service or is discharged honorably. Amazingly enough, there is a record of at least one man who exonerated himself in this way and is now buried in Arlington.

4. Discharge from the draft

A person who, although he may have been ordered to report to an induction station, but was not actually inducted into the military service, is not eligible for burial at Arlington.

THE TYPES OF MILITARY
FUNERALS

THERE are three basic types of military funerals—Full Honors, Modified Honors and Body Bearers Only with no honors provided.

Every serviceman is entitled to a Full Honors ceremony if his family requests it, although most do not. The number of flourishes alters with rank but the fundamental procedures remain the same.

1. The Full Honors funeral

The basics of a Full Honors military funeral for any serviceman include the flag draped over the casket, a military escort, the rendering of honors and salutes, appropriate religious services, firing squad, taps, and the presentation of the colors to the next of kin.

The size of the official escort is prescribed by the rank of the deceased. The following designations are for Navy funerals. The Army and the Air Force follow similar procedures for the appropriate ranks.

For admirals, the escort includes an escort commander and adjutant, a band, two platoons of Marines (one officer and 25 enlisted men in each), colors and color guards, two platoons of bluejackets (same number as Marines), eight-man firing squad and petty officer, personal flag bearer and ushers. For commanders and captains, the official escort includes an escort commander (and adjutant for a captain), a band, two platoons of bluejackets, eight-man firing squad, colors and color guard, body bearers and ushers.

For ensigns through lieutenant commanders (including midshipmen and warrant officers) the official escort includes an escort commander, a band, one platoon of bluejackets, colors and color guard, body bearers and ushers.

For chief petty officers, the official escort includes two squads of bluejackets (eight men in each), body bearers, ushers and a bugler.

For enlisted men the official escort includes one squad of bluejackets, body bearers, ushers and a bugler.

When an escort commander is used, he must be the same rank or higher than the deceased. In the case of captains or higher, the escort commander's function is largely symbolic. A Ceremonial Guard officer acts as adjutant and actually gives all of the commands.

The most complete procession for a general or admiral rank would follow this outline:

Escort commander
Adjutant
Marine detachment
National colors
Navy detachment
Chaplain
Personal flag
Caisson flanked by honorary pallbearers
Body bearers
Caparisoned horse (if authorized)
Members of the immediate family
Enlisted men from the command of the deceased
Officers from the command of the deceased
Official delegations
Societies, professional or social

2. Modified Honors

The next of kin may request any of the above listed honors to be omitted from the ceremony as they desire.

3. Body Bearers Only

This is for a purely civilian ceremony where no honors are rendered and no flag is used. The conventions for a regular civilian funeral ceremony apply.

The question of music is largely left to the family. The United States Army band at Fort Myer has an extensive repertoire of the more usual musical offerings for a military funeral. The band maintains a policy of trying to accommodate family requests and requires only that the suggested music be "in keeping with the solemnity of the military service."*

The suggested list of music includes the following:

Moving the deceased into the chapel—"Lead Kindly Light."

Moving the deceased outside of the chapel "Abide with Me."

During the procession to the grave (in order) "R. G. Hall," "Marche Funèbre" by Beethoven, "Pontificale" march, "March Religioso," and "God of Our Fathers."

Removing the casket from the caisson at the grave— "Nearer My God to Thee" Protestant), "Holy God We Praise Thy Name" (Roman Catholic), "Eternal Father" (nondenominational).

Boxing the flag—"America the Beautiful."

* As the band has only about 48 hours notice prior to any individual burial ceremony, it cannot meet every request for a selection that is not already in its repertoire. However, if outstanding commitments permit rehearsal time, the band has been known to master a new arrangement on such short notice.

APPENDIX C

DISTINGUISHED AMERICANS WHOSE REMAINS HAVE LAIN IN STATE AT THE CAPITOL ON THE HISTORIC CATAFALQUE

Abraham Lincoln	1865
President of the United States	
Thaddeus Stevens	1868
Representative from Pennsylvania	
Charles Sumner	1874
Senator from Massachusetts	
James Garfield	1881
President of the United States	
Major General John Logan	1886
Civil War General and Senator from Illinois	
William McKinley	1901
President of the United States	
Major Pierre L'Enfant	1909*
Engineer-Planner of Washington, D.C.	
Admiral George Dewey	1917
Hero of the Battle of Manila Bay	
The Unknown Soldier (World War I)	1921
Warren Harding	1923
President of the United States	

* On the occasion of his reinterment in Arlington National Cemetery.

William Howard Taft	1930
President and Chief Justice of the United States	
General John J. Pershing	1948
Commander of the AEF	
Robert Taft	1953
Senator from Ohio	
The Unknowns of World War II and Korea	1958
John F. Kennedy	1963
President of the United States	

BIOGRAPHICAL SKETCHES

General Henry H. Arnold
(1886–1950)

IN contrast to his well-known nickname "Hap," acquired during West Point days for his sunny disposition, the general was also known as "Do It Yesterday" Arnold. As commanding general of the United States Air Force in World War II, in charge of two and a half million men and 75,000 aircraft, he not infrequently put in eighteen- to twenty-four-hour working days. If he was happy, he was not go-lucky.

Henry Harley Arnold was born in Gladwyne, Pennsylvania, on June 25, 1886, the son of H. A. and Louise Harley Arnold. After graduating from West Point in 1907, the young second lieutenant was assigned to the Philippines, then to an infantry detachment on Governor's Island, New York. He was ordered to Dayton, Ohio, in 1911, for flight training with the Wright brothers and eventually became the twenty-ninth pilot to be licensed in the United States.

The Signal Corps at that time had five planes and an annual aviation budget of $125,000, but Lieutenant Arnold soon began to make the most of their meager resources. In 1912 he set an altitude record of 6,540 feet and in the same year won the Mackay Trophy for a thirty-mile flight from College Park, Maryland, to Fort Myer, Virginia, and back, in an early Wright biplane with a forty-horsepower engine revolving two propellers with a chain-and-sprocket device. During the flight he observed a troop of cavalry and became the first man to make aerial reports of military observations by wireless. Twenty-three years later, he won the prized trophy again for commanding a squadron of ten bombers on a flight from Washington, D.C., to Fairbanks, Alaska, and back.

In 1913, he married Eleanor Pool, and they raised three sons and a daughter.

When the United States entered World War I, Lieutenant Arnold was in Panama and set to work organizing and commanding the 7th Aeronautical Squadron, an air defense unit. As a result he served only a few months overseas. He also worked as the assistant director of the Office of Military Aeronautics, bossing thirty training schools, 15,000 officers and 125,000 enlisted men. Like Billy Mitchell and Hermann Göring, he became convinced from experiences in the First World War that air power would be a decisive factor in future wars. He was known as a "Mitchell man" but kept his mouth shut when espousal of aviation causes was not politic and moved ahead when the climate was better.

Arnold was graduated from the Army Industrial College in 1925, and the Command and Staff School at Fort Leavenworth, Kansas, in 1929. His career then moved into high gear. From 1931, in seven years he strode from lieutenant colonel to major general, from commander of March Field in California to Air Force assistant chief to chief in 1938. After the attack on Pearl Harbor he was a lieutenant general in command of all American air forces. Later that same year he won the Distinguished Service Medal for leading a seventy-seven-hour flight from Brisbane to San Francisco. He was made the first full aviation general in 1943, and in 1944 President Truman elevated him, along with Generals Marshall, Eisenhower and MacArthur, to five-star general of the Army.

Five-Star General Arnold was always popular with his men. He was noted not only for his amiability but also for an encyclopedic memory for aviation facts—not altogether surprising for the man with the longest record of continuous flying in the Army. Arnold liked to recall the story of the scar on his chin, a memento of an offshore ditch landing he was forced to make in the Atlantic in 1912. Arnold clung to the wing of his wrecked plane and watched helplessly while two dour old men dressed in faded Union Army uniforms rowed past but refused to rescue him because they didn't approve of airplanes or the people who flew in them.

1944 also saw the establishment of the famed 20th Air Force in the Pacific. Composed entirely of B-29's, this strategic striking group was kept under Arnold's personal command until the end of the war. During the summer of 1945 the 20th unloaded as much as 5,500 tons of blockbusters on Japanese cities every day. Arnold retired in January, 1946, and was succeeded by his long-time friend, General Carl Spaatz. Four years later, on January 15, 1950, Arnold died in Sonoma, California.

Stephen Vincent Benét
(1898–1943)

WHEN young poet Steve Benét was discovered as a freshman at Yale in 1915 by a clique of literary sophomores, it was said that he "needed a haircut, was using language coarse beyond the limits of Yale's currently muscular Christianity, and was pitching pennies on the stone floor with unsuitable companions." From this inauspicious beginning he went on to become one of the best-known and best-liked men at Yale, arguing heatedly, drinking heavily (he once lay in a snowbank outside Mory's until rescued and carried home), and writing with amazing speed, inventiveness, and fecundity.

He was born in Bethlehem, Pennsylvania, on July 22, 1898, of an Army family. His great-grandfather, grandfather and father were career officers; the latter two, West Point men. His grandfather, Brigadier General Stephen Vincent Benét, rose to become chief of Ordnance. The poet was proud of this military heritage and once said, "My grandfather developed the rim-fire cartridge; my father was in charge of the first 16-inch gun ever made in this country; and my uncle helped invent one of the earliest light machine guns, the Benét-Mercier."

His childhood, spent in various Army posts, was happy, marred only by frequent illnesses. An attack of scarlet fever permanently damaged his eyesight and kept him from entering West Point. He was precocious and bookish, reading extensively and constantly, even while bicycling.

Benét wrote furiously all during his teens. By seventeen he had published his first book (written on six successive Sundays), and he wrote his second at nineteen. His college career was marked by continued immersion in writing anything, anytime, anywhere. Indeed, writing was the only thing he ever worked at. When World War I came, he tried repeatedly to join the Army but was refused because of bad eyesight. Finally (as did Ernest Hemingway) he memorized the eye chart and was accepted, but was discharged three days later when a sergeant caught him trying to peel a potato he could barely see.

After a master's degree at Yale, graduate work at the Sorbonne, marriage in 1921, which later produced two daughters and a son, Benét received a Guggenheim Fellowship that took him to Paris in 1926, where one year he wrote "John Brown's Body," the monumental Civil War poem which won him the Pulitzer Prize in 1929. This was followed in 1937 by his great prose success, "The Devil and Daniel Webster." Benét, a tall, balding, mustached, thick-spectacled figure in a rumpled Brooks Brothers suit, constantly drew on his deep knowledge and love of Americana, evoking rich images with deceptive simplicity of language.

A gregarious man, he was an indefatigable letter-writer, and even a partial list of his friends and correspondents would suffice as an introduction to the literary lions of the day: Sinclair Lewis, Christopher Morley, Archibald Mac-Leish, Christopher LaFarge, Edna St. Vincent Millay, Van Wyck Brooks, Douglas Southall Freeman.

He continued to write, up through World War II, turning out an incredible number of poems, novels, prefaces, reviews, criticisms, reader's reports, operas, radio plays. He even spent a brief, unhappy stint in Hollywood writing a screenplay on Lincoln, for D. W. Griffith. As the war mounted, Benét turned more and more to the radio play, working with a fiery patriotism to produce whatever he thought would help the war effort, always without pay. Nothing seemed too much to tackle, and while his innumerable contributions gained for him even greater fame and the gratitude of a nation at war (he even had a Liberty Ship named for him), the workload sapped his never robust health at an alarming rate. Finally, in the early morning hours of March 13, 1943, he suffered a heart attack and died a few minutes later in his wife's arms.

William Jennings Bryan
(1860–1925)

WHEN President Wilson offered William Jennings Bryan the
post of Secretary of State in 1913, Bryan asked Wilson if his
abstemious habits would prove "an insurmountable obstacle"
to his filling the office. Assured that they would not, Bryan
accepted. Later, at an official diplomatic reception he served
only water and grape juice to the thirsty guests, because he
thought the water glasses "looked a little lonesome."

This blend of staunch Presbyterianism and wry humor was
characteristic of the man known variously as the "Peerless
Leader," "Son of the Middle Border," but probably best as
"The Great Commoner."

He was born on March 19, 1860, in Salem, Illinois, the son
of a circuit court judge and a strong-minded, religious
mother. His education owed as much to *McGuffey's Reader*,
Horatio Alger, and the Bible as it did to the academy and
colleges he attended. Graduating as valedictorian from Chicago's Union College of Law in 1883, he opened his own law
office in Illinois in the same year, on July 4, because of a
fondness for important dates. Bearded at the time, he was in
later life a clean-shaven, tall, firm-jawed man with piercing
eyes, whose flowing mane became a male tonsorial fad.

Bryan married in 1884, and three years later moved his
practice to Nebraska, where his integrity, deep populist sym-

pathies and formidable oratorical gifts brought him election to Congress and the editorship of an Omaha newspaper.

At the Democratic convention in the Chicago Coliseum on July 9, 1896, he delivered the famous "Cross of Gold" speech ("You shall not crucify mankind upon a cross of gold"), advocating a national monetary silver standard; and at thirty-six, he was nominated for the Presidency. After an 18,000-mile campaign, prodigious for his day, he was defeated by prosperous times and William McKinley in November.

During the Spanish-American War, Colonel Bryan served briefly as commander of the Third Nebraska Volunteers, resigning the day the treaty was signed. His claim to military glory lay in his military title, bestowed by the governor of Nebraska, and in serving under Major General Fitzhugh Lee, nephew of Robert E. Lee.

His ascendancy in the Democratic party still undiminished, he ran for President again in 1900, with Adlai Stevenson as his running mate, but was once again defeated by McKinley.

Bryan's vast popular appeal stemmed not only from his "silver tongue" but from his implicit faith in people, in the virtue of physical labor, in the efficacy of free elections, legislation, the two-party system, and in radical change. "The conservative is necessary to keep the radical from going too far," he said, "but the radical is necessary to make the conservative go at all."

After countless Chautauqua lectures, continuous publication of his writing, unremitting political activity and a much publicized world tour during which he met his idol, Tolstoy, Bryan was nominated for the Presidency yet a third time, in 1908. William Howard Taft defeated him and from then on his hitherto undisputed political power suffered a relative decline, though his support in the 1912 Democratic convention helped nominate Wilson.

As Secretary of State, his undistinguished two-year tenure was clouded by charges of pacifism owing to his arbitration-minded views over the *Lusitania* sinking, and he resigned the day Wilson signed the second and decisive protest note.

Probably the darkest days of William Jennings Bryan's life occurred some years later during the Scopes Monkey Trial at Dayton, Tennessee. Sick and enfeebled, he assisted in the prosecution of a schoolteacher charged with teaching Darwinian theories of evolution, but was made to appear a gallus-snapping, Fundamentalist, old fool by the rip-saw forensics of his opponent for the defense, Clarence Darrow. Five days after the trial's end, in Dayton, Ohio, on July 26, 1925, the Great Commoner died in his sleep.

Admiral Richard E. Byrd

(1888–1957)

FEW MEN have ever received more honors during their lifetime than did Admiral Byrd. The Congressional Medal of
Honor after his historic flight over the North Pole in 1926
and the Order of Merit in 1945 were among the many
decorations, promotions, and accolades, public and private,
bestowed upon him by a grateful nation for his numerous
contributions in military, scientific, and humanitarian fields.

Richard Evelyn Byrd was born October 25, 1888, in Winchester, Virginia, the younger brother of United States Senator Harry Byrd, and a descendant of William Byrd, a wealthy
colonial planter and public official. His adult resourcefulness
was foreshadowed when, as a boy of twelve, he took an
unescorted trip around the world. He attended the Shenandoah Valley Military Academy, Virginia Military Institute,
and the University of Virginia, before entering the United
States Naval Academy and graduating from there in 1912. An
academy sports injury forced his retirement from active service three years later, after assignments at sea and at Guantanamo, Cuba. He reentered the Navy during World War I,
took flight training, and served as commander of United
States Aviation in Canada, thereafter continuing to gravitate
to administrative posts. After the war he was active in developing plans for transatlantic flight by airplanes and diri-

gibles, gave navigational training to Charles Lindbergh, and himself made a crossing in 1927, but was forced by foul weather to ditch the plane off the coast of France.

Byrd's polar career began in 1924 when he accompanied Commander McMillan's expedition to western Greenland. He subsequently organized a private expedition to King's Bay, Spitsbergen, and on May 9, 1926, in his trimotor plane, the *Josephine Ford*, he made the first flight over the North Pole. Following all this, he had little trouble in later organizing support for a southern expedition, and in December, 1928, he established his forty-two-man Little America base at Bay of Whales, Antarctica. From there, he made the first flight over the South Pole on November 29, 1929. Shortly afterward, in 1930, the rank of rear admiral was conferred upon him.

Four years later he returned to Little America with a fifty-six-man expedition in order to extend exploration and scientific observation. That year of 1934, Admiral Byrd set up a small hut at Bolling advanced base, 123 miles south of the main base, and under incredible hardship spent the polar winter entirely alone. At one point, for example, he measured and found that the sub-zero temperature was 30° colder at his feet than at his head. After five months, during which he nearly died of carbon monoxide fumes, he was relieved by an unrequested "rescue" party. He had established man's farthest-south and Antarctica's only inland habitation for the next twenty-one years.

Byrd made successive trips to the area as director of expeditions and Government Antarctic programs, exploring, mapping, photographing. During World War II he lent invaluable assistance to naval staff operations in evaluating island landing sites, and in 1954 he was appointed head of the

United States Navy Operation Deepfreeze, a contribution to the International Geophysical Year of 1957–58. In this connection he made several flights to the area and last flew over the South Pole January 8, 1956. Ill health prevented his seeing the operation to its conclusion, and he died in Boston, March 11, 1957. He was buried with full military honors at Arlington Cemetery.

A lean, silver-haired, handsome man, Richard Byrd epitomized the distinguished man of action, in looks and bearing. In addition, he possessed a fine mind and invented several instruments of great value in aerial navigation, including a bubble sextant, a sun compass, and a drift indicator. Besides frequently contributing to the *National Geographic,* he authored four books, the best known of which was the account of his solitary polar sojourn, *Alone,* published in 1938.

General Claire Chennault
(1890–1958)

"Old Leatherface," his men called him, and "The Old Man," and even "God." Chennault was a stern leader and a tough, daring, and canny fighter. His tatterdemalion "Flying Tigers" chalked up a World War II record of ten Japanese planes destroyed to every one of theirs, and General Takahashi, commander of Japanese forces in Central China, later said of Chennault's wartime 14th Air Force that it constituted "seventy-five percent of all effective opposition," and that, had it not been for them, he could have "gone anywhere."

Claire Lee Chennault sprang from Huguenot ancestors who came with Lafayette to fight for American independence. He was born in Commerce, Texas, September 6, 1890, to John Stonewall Jackson Chennault and the former Jessie Lee, cousin to Robert E. Lee. Young Claire spent a Huck Finn boyhood in rural Louisiana before attending Louisiana University. Upon graduation he taught at a rural school where his first day's duties included thrashing the biggest boy in class, larger than himself.

He joined the Army in World War I and after officers' training at Fort Benjamin Harrison, Indiana, he entered the aviation section of the signal Corps, then transferred in 1920 to the Army Air Service as a first lieutenant. Chennault soon made himself an expert in air warfare tactics, publishing many sound, but far-advanced, theories that went largely unheeded. During 1930, he earned a reputation for skill and fearlessness as the leader of a flying stunt and tactics group known as the "Three Men on a Flying Trapeze."

In 1937, the then Captain Chennault was reluctantly retired from the Air Force for deafness, but he immediately accepted Chiang Kai-shek's offer to come to China and reorganize his tiny air force while training Chinese pilots to man it. This he did for three years until America's entry into World War II, whereupon he embarked upon a vigorous recruitment of crack American flyers for his famed "Flying Tigers," leading them in their storybook exploits in defense of China, with particular attention to keeping the vital Burma Road open. The Air Force recalled him to active service as a brigadier general in 1942, and a year later made him a major general and commander of the 14th Air Force in China. His brilliant leadership and superior tactics succeeded in offsetting the inferior numbers and equipment of his own forces, amid the conflict arising from General "Vinegar Joe" Stilwell's distrust of Chiang Kai-shek. This imbroglio eventually led to Chennault's replacement and retirement in 1945.

After the war, upon terminating an earlier marriage, Chennault married Anna Chang, a beautiful Chinese journalist, daughter of China's consul general in San Francisco. Though she was thirty years his junior, it was an exceptionally happy marriage, and they had two daughters, to whom Madame Chiang Kai-shek served as godmother.

Chennault returned to China in 1946 to organize the Civil Air Transport for the generalissimo, and directed the organization on Formosa until 1958 when he returned to America for treatment of lung cancer. Despite a game and sanguine fight against the disease, Chennault succumbed in New Orleans, July 27, 1958, nine days after receiving the third star of a lieutenant general. He was buried with full military honors at Arlington Cemetery.

General Chennault was a lithe, wiry man of a commanding presence, with a jut-jawed, granitelike face that once moved Winston Churchill to remark, "What a face! Thank God he's on our side." His firm ideas of duty and fierce competitiveness were tempered with an active sense of humor; his favorite method of silencing an over-loquacious dinner guest was to press upon him fiery Louisiana red peppers which he himself would be chewing with no visible effect.

His publications include the autobiographical *Way of a Fighter*, published in 1949.

General John Clem
(1851–1937)

As the youngest soldier ever to bear arms in a major war, "Johnny Shiloh" apparently had ideas later of becoming one of the oldest. During World War I, the nearly seventy-year-old officer requested permission to go abroad and fight with the AEF. To his disappointment, President Wilson flatly refused him.

He was born John Joseph Klem in Newark, Ohio, on August 31, 1851, son of German immigrants Roman and Magdalene. At the height of the Presidential election of 1860, the patriotic lad changed his middle name to Lincoln. On May 24th of the following year, shortly after the death of his beloved mother, he ran away to enlist in the fighting, and became, at ten, a drummer boy with the Union army.

The doughty little figure soon became a legend, had two ponies shot out from under him and was wounded three times. He won his most commonly used sobriquet, "Johnny Shiloh," for his performance at the Battle of Pittsburg near Shiloh Meeting House, was known variously as "The Drummer Boy of Shiloh," "Johnny Chickamauga," and "The Drummer Boy of Chickamauga."

After the Battle of Pittsburg, he advanced from drummer boy to marker, then to orderly sergeant with the army of the Cumberland under General George Thomas, who took a paternal interest in the little soldier. He fought at the battles of Perryville, Murfreesboro, Lookout Mountain, Missionary Ridge, Kennesaw Mountain, Resaca, Peachtree Creek and Atlanta; later he received a second lieutenant's commission from the hands of President Grant, an old and close wartime friend.

His military career came to an end for all practical purposes with President Wilson's refusal and he retired as a major general to San Antonio, where he lived quietly until his death there May 13, 1937.

Just when John Joseph Klem began to sign his name John Lincoln Clem is not clear. He managed to impose his middle name upon the War Department, but was not allowed the "C" spelling. His official papers in the National Archives in Washington are known as the John L. Clem Papers, though the papers themselves carry the spelling Klem.

It is "The Drummer Boy of Chickamauga" which is engraved on the monument over his grave at Arlington Cemetery, where he is buried near another wartime friend, General Phil Sheridan.

General George Crook
(1829–1890)

GENERAL SHERMAN called him "the greatest Indian fighter the United States Army ever had."

George Crook, born the ninth of ten children on September 8, 1829, to a prosperous farmer near Taylorville, Ohio, entered West Point in 1848. His career there was outstanding only for the fact that he was the lowest-ranking graduate ever to be promoted to major general.

As a newly commissioned lieutenant of infantry, he was sent to the Northwest where he spent the years protecting settlers from Indian raids. In 1861 he was brought back as colonel in command of the 36th Ohio Infantry to begin serving with Union forces in West Virginia. His brilliant, utterly fearless conduct throughout the war brought him repeated promotions until 1864 when he was placed in personal command of a corps of Sheridan's Army of the Shenandoah and received the brevet of major general of Volunteers and regular Army.

Crook's frontier experience was invaluable in his special effectiveness with the swift foray, disrupting rail communications, cleaning out nests of Confederate "bushwhackers." He fought the campaigns of Antietam, Chickamauga, and the last battles of the war through Appomattox.

In the postwar Army reorganization, Crook was sent as a

lieutenant colonel of Infantry to command the Boise, Idaho, region, where he put an end to the long, agonizing Indian war. President Grant then asked him in 1871 to proceed to northern Arizona to pacify the Apaches and other insurgents. He did this with such resounding success that he was promoted to brigadier general, highly unusual advancement for the time. His next command was the Department of the Platte where he led the United States forces in the Great Sioux War of 1876. He fought against Sitting Bull and Crazy Horse. On June 17, the anniversary of Bull Run, he suffered his only major defeat at the hands of the Indians, who outnumbered him three to one, at the Battle of Rosebud River. This was eight days before Custer's disaster at the Little Big Horn. Perhaps significantly, it is at this point that Crook ends his autobiography (discovered only in 1942 tucked away in the War College Library in Washington, D.C.

1882 found him again in Arizona, back battling his old enemy, the Apaches, this time on the warpath under the redoubtable Geronimo. The murderous fighting was culminated when Crook led an expedition into the Sierra Madre, where no white man had been before, and persuaded the holed-up band of several hundred hostile Indians to return to the reservation.

A few years later he was made major general in command of the Division of Missouri, with headquarters in Chicago, where he died on March 21, 1890.

Throughout his life, Crook, a man of middle height with a flowing, patriarchal beard, was known for his great personal courage and modesty. He was laconic ("Example is always the best general order"), abstemious, startlingly nonprofane for a frontier soldier, sharply critical of the licentiousness, greed and drunkenness he saw on the plains, contemptuous of suspected cowardice and sloth in fellow officers, compassionate for others' misfortunes, and uncomplaining of his own (he carried an arrowhead in his hip, to the grave). He always regarded Indian fighting as a profession, though he did not enjoy killing. Crook understood Indians and their customs, spoke several dialects, and as an administrator was more inclined to pardon than to punish. He became a leading exponent of reform in Indian affairs.

Upon Crook's death, Red Cloud, Chief of the Sioux, said in epitaph, "He, at least, had never lied to us."

General William Donovan
(1883–1959)

GENERAL WILLIAM "WILD BILL" DONOVAN was one of those rarest of avis—an authentic original. It is hard to believe that America will ever again see anything like the meteor that was General Donovan. Born of poor Irish immigrants on New Year's Day of 1883, in Buffalo, New York, Donovan was to become the most highly decorated man in the history of American public service. He was the only person to hold the four highest awards America can offer—the Congressional Medal of Honor, the Distinguished Service Cross, the Distinguished Service Medal and the National Security Medal.

Commander of the famed Fighting 69th during World War I, Donovan won his CMH during the Meuse-Argonne offensive. Gravely wounded in the legs, Donovan had himself carried into battle and directed a bloody bayonet and hand grenade charge. The mild-mannered Donovan with his soft, lilting Irish voice and unmilitary bearing, picked up his lifetime sobriquet one day when he was chaffing his men for looking tired after a hard day of maneuvers.

"I have fifty pounds on my back, the same as you do," Donovan told them, "and I'm twenty years older than any of you boys."

"Yeah," a voice wafted back from the ranks, "but we ain't no wild man like you, Bill"—and "Wild Bill" it remained.

After amassing a sizable fortune as an international lawyer

and helping to found the American Legion, Donovan was called back into service by President Roosevelt shortly before America's entry into World War II. He operated first as FDR's personal envoy to Europe during the dark days of the seemingly unstoppable German advance. When most of Roosevelt's other advisors were pessimistically suggesting that the best England could hope for was evacuation to Canada, it was Donovan's energetic voice which expressed the confidence that England could last out the blitz.

On June 18, 1941, FDR handed Donovan his toughest assignment: to create a strategic intelligence organization for the United States.

"You'll have to start with nothing," Roosevelt said, "we have no intelligence system at all."

Donovan carved out the famous OSS (Office of Strategic Services). His reign as head of the OSS was marked by the extravagant exuberance he brought to everything he ever did. When he learned the service had just perfected a new completely silent pistol, the delighted Donovan marched straight into Roosevelt's office with it while the President was busy dictating. Without saying a word Donovan dropped a sandbag on the floor, stood back and emptied the pistol into it without the secretary ever realizing what was happening.

Donovan was everywhere. He landed behind enemy lines in Burma, "to see how my fellows are getting along," and flew dozens of top secret and highly dangerous missions. Although it was against all orders, he sneaked ashore at Normandy on D-Day. He was supposed to have the famous OSS lethal pill with him against possible capture, but found he had brought his aspirin by mistake. Excitement without worrying about details was the General's forte.

From July, 1941, until he was named brigidier general in

April, 1943, he drew no salary at all. Told by President Roosevelt to put in an expense account to cover a personal outlay the general had made for OSS business, Donovan submitted one for $1,000. But when the Treasury Department told him that it had to be itemized, he withdrew it and never bothered to put in another one for the rest of his career.

The General was retired almost immediately after V-J Day, but he could not stay out of public service. After turning down a number of opportunities for first rank ambassadorial posts he finally agreed to be the United States envoy to Thailand in 1953, because he thought it was the toughest assignment available at the time. He was seventy years old. In 1956 he organized a refugee relief committee which raised more than $1.5 million to aid the freedom fighters escaping from the tragically abortive Budapest uprisings.

Finally the hero's heart, which first served under the American colors in the Mexican campaigns in 1916, faltered. He died in Walter Reed Hospital on February 8, 1959.

Abner Doubleday

(1819–1893)

IT is ironic that the man whom popular tradition credits with having invented the "national pastime," baseball, should be so little known generally for his military deeds, which were noteworthy and rested upon considerably firmer historical ground than the irrepressible but largely apocryphal sports legend.

Abner Doubleday, one of three sons, was born at Ballston Spa, New York, June 26, 1819. He came of Huguenot ancestry, the family name having originally been Dubaldy. He attended school at Auburn and at Cooperstown, where he prepared for a career in civil engineering.

It was while he was in school at Cooperstown that he is said to have created baseball, in 1839. The town is the site of baseball's national Hall of Fame and the original playing field is now a public playground called Doubleday Field. It is likely that Doubleday did add some modifications and form to the chaos of existing bat-and-ball games, such as the insistence upon a diamond-shaped playing field and assignment of definite positions to players, and he had eleven men to a team. A baseball high commission, including two United States senators and headed by Albert G. Spaulding for whom the commission was named, spent from 1900 to 1907 investigating the origins of the game and at last pronounced Dou-

Major Pierre Charles L'Enfant

General George Crook

General Philip Kearney

General Abner Doubleday

General Philip H. Sheridan

General John Clem

Robert Todd Lincoln

Chief Justice
Oliver Wendell Holmes

Admiral Robert E. Peary

William Jennings Bryan

Major Walter Reed

William Howard Taft

General John J. Pershing

Stephen Vincent Benét

General William J. Donovan

Admiral Richard E. Byrd

General Jonathan M. Wainwright

General George C. Marshall

General Claire L. Chennault

General Henry H. Arnold

Above left
Admiral William D. Leahy

Above right
Admiral Marc Mitscher

Left
Admiral William F. Halsey, Jr.

Above left
James V. Forrestal

Above right
John Foster Dulles

Right
Medgar Evers

John Fitzgerald Kennedy

bleday its inventor. Sports scholars, however, have unearthed sources where the term "baseball" was used as much as a hundred years before 1839. Some have even gone back so far as to cite a certain Thomas Wilson, a clergyman of Maidstone, England, who in 1700 decried "cudgell-playing, baseball and cricketts on the Lord's Day." Authorities generally now subscribe to Henry Chadwick's thesis that baseball is an offshoot of the early English game of rounders, itself an offshoot of cricket. But legend is stronger than history and Abner Doubleday remains the father of baseball.

Doubleday was appointed a cadet at West Point in 1838, graduating in 1842 to a commission in the artillery. He served with the army of Zachary Taylor engaging in the Battle of Monterey, and later fought in Florida during the Seminole War of 1856–58. The remainder of his service before the Civil War was spent in posts along the Atlantic coast, as he rose to be first lieutenant in 1847 and captain in 1855.

As an artillery officer and second in command of the Union garrison, he fired the first shot from Fort Sumter in response to the Confederate bombardment. His aim was good, but the shot "bounced off from the sloping roof of the (ironclad) battery opposite without any effect."

In May, 1861, he was assigned as a major with the newly organized 17th Infantry and served in the lower Shenandoah Valley and in the defense of Washington before being appointed brigadier general of Volunteers in February, 1862. He took command of a brigade in McDowell's corps with the Army of the Potomac and saw action on the Rappahannock and the second Battle of Bull Run. When the chief of his division was wounded, he succeeded to its command and took it into battle at Antietam and Fredericksburg. He became a major general of Volunteers in November, 1862.

The battle of Gettysburg brought Doubleday his greatest distinction and his greatest disappointment. The first day's fighting was waged by whatever pick-up troops were available to hold back the Confederates until full Union strength could be brought up. When General Reynolds was killed in the confused battle, Doubleday gallantly commanded the I Corps through a day of desperate fighting against heavy odds. He felt he had fairly earned permanent command, but when Newton (his classmate at West Point) was assigned to take charge that night, and he was returned to head his division, Doubleday felt deeply humiliated. He never forgave General Meade, who had made the assignment without full knowledge of the facts.

Gettysburg was his last combat service and he spent the rest of the war on duty in Washington. He was promoted to colonel in 1867, left the Army in 1873, and spent twenty years in retirement at Mendham, New Jersey, where he died June 26, 1893.

Doubleday was tall, full-mustached, distinguished in appearance and courteous in manner. He abjured profanity, tobacco, and liquor, and his methodical and deliberate ways earned him the nickname "Forty-eight Hours." A man of wide interests, he spent his last years indulging his fondness, acquired as a boy, for French and Spanish literature and the study of Sanskrit. He also wrote two important books on the Civil War: *Reminiscences of Forts Sumter and Moultrie in 1860–61* and *Chancellorsville and Gettysburg*. A bronze statue in his memory was unveiled at Gettysburg in 1917.

John Foster Dulles
(1888–1959)

PROBABLY no man ever came to the office of Secretary of State bearing more impressive credentials than Dulles. He was the grandson of John Watson Foster, the Secretary under President Benjamin Harrison, and the nephew of Robert Lansing, the Secretary under President Wilson. He had himself served as advisor to politicians, as a senator, as a State Department consultant, and as a delegate to peace conferences and to the United Nations.

He was born February 25, 1888 in Washington, D.C., to the liberal Presbyterian minister Reverend Allen Macy Dulles and the former Edith Foster, whose family traced its genealogy straight back to Charlemagne. The boy grew up in Watertown, New York in a strictly religious home, though he was equally exposed to secular affairs with frequent visits by diplomats and politicians and family trips to Europe. During his youth, Dulles was active in outdoor sports and developed the physical toughness and love of sailing that lasted throughout his life. Expecting to enter the ministry, he majored in philosophy at Princeton and graduated Phi Beta Kappa valedictorian. His senior thesis won him a year's scholarship to the Sorbonne where he studied philosophy under Bergson.

While still a junior in college, Dulles got his first real taste of international diplomacy in 1907 when he attended The

Hague Peace Conference. With his fluency in French, he worked as interpreter for the Chinese delegation.

Upon his return from the Sorbonne, Dulles opted for the law and soon entered George Washington University. In a hectic two years, he completed three years' work with the highest marks ever made there, but through a technicality was denied a degree.

He secured his first position with his grandfather's old law firm in New York. His knowledge of Spanish led to handling the firm's interests in Latin America, and on one trip he nearly died of malaria. The massive doses of quinine attacked his optic nerve, leaving him with impaired vision and a tic in the left eye. In 1912, still convalescing, Dulles married Janet Avery, and took a nurse along on their honeymoon. His marriage was happy and produced a daughter and two sons, the younger of whom became a Jesuit priest.

When World War I began, the rising young lawyer was barred from active service because of poor eyesight but was commissioned a captain, later a major, to serve on the War Trade Board. After the armistice, he attended the Versailles Peace Conference, and performed impressively as legal counsel to the American delegation of the Commission on Reparations.

Succeeding years saw him shuttling back and forth to Europe on business, becoming at thirty-eight a senior partner of his firm, a director of fifteen corporations, and one of the dozen highest paid lawyers in the world. Always an extremely active lay churchman, Dulles also became increasingly interested in international affairs, published the philosophical *War, Peace, and Change* in 1939, and was later Presidential candidate Thomas Dewey's foreign policy advisor.

In July, 1949, Governor Dewey called Dulles away from

the primitive retreat on his privately owned Duck Island in Lake Ontario. The ailing New York Republican Senator Wagner had just resigned and the governor named his old associate to finish the term. Allying himself with fellow internationalist Senator Vandenberg of Michigan, he took to his senatorial role with zest; but when he stood for reelection the following November the publicly unimpressive Dulles was handily defeated by Democratic ex-Governor Lehman.

Early in 1950, he was appointed consultant to the State Department and masterminded the writing of the peace treaty with Japan. A superbly craftsmanlike job, it took a year to write and embodied Dulles' concepts of "a just and durable peace."

After working hard for General Eisenhower's election to the Presidency in 1952, Dulles was entrusted with the office he had long wanted and for which he could almost be said to have been heading since youth. As Eisenhower's first cabinet appointee, John Foster Dulles was sworn in as Secretary of State the day after the Presidential inauguration in 1953.

Dulles was among the most controversial Secretaries in history. Though none doubted his inherent ability, he alienated many. At times, direct to the point of bluntness, at others, his lawyer's methods could prompt the observation that he "does not always move in a straight line to his goal." Intellectually vain, he was not proud personally, wearing his Savile Row suits slightly rumpled, and once gravely receiving importunate visitors while sitting in the bathtub in his hotel suite. Aides called him "Foster" and he had a habit of whittling with his penknife during conferences, which unsettled many and particularly irritated Molotov.

A long-time student, and enemy, of communism, he kept a copy of Stalin's *Problems of Leninism* on his desk, along with the *Federalist Papers* and the Bible. He constantly preached total collective security for the United States and its allies and advocated massive retaliation as a deterrent to war. Three times during his tenure, the United States "marched to the brink of war," and the coinage "brinkmanship," which he called a "necessary art," was always associated with him.

Known as the most traveled Secretary of State in history, Dulles made sixty trips covering a half-million miles in the six years of his office. With his characteristic courage and resolution, he continued his heavy schedule until the last, in the face of his knowledge that he was carrying a malignant tumor. Finally, he was forced to resign April 15, 1959, less than six weeks prior to his death in Washington on May 24.

Medgar Evers
(1925–1963)

"I expect to be shot," once said Medgar Evers prophetically, "I might die. But that's the risk." The Mississippi Field Secretary of the National Association for the Advancement of Colored People, later slain by a shot in the back, had just been offered a job at national NAACP headquarters in New York, but refused, saying, "The fight is here."

Medgar Wiley Evers was born July 2, 1925, in Decatur, Mississippi, and attended segregated elementary and high schools in Newton County, then enlisted in the army in 1943. He participated in the Normandy invasion and campaign in northern France, and received two Bronze Stars before being discharged in 1946.

The new veteran enrolled in Mississippi's all-Negro Alcorn A & M College, majoring in business administration, and became an insurance salesman after graduation.

Evers played four years of varsity football in college, and there met his future wife, Myrlie Beasley, whom he married in 1951. They had three children, the eldest a son named Darrell Kenyatta, after the African leader Jomo Kenyatta.

As a boy of fourteen, young Medgar had watched a neighboring Negro man lynched, and he carried the memories with him throughout his life. He was the first Negro to attempt to enroll in the University of Mississippi; later, he actively helped James Meredith in his successful entry into that previously all-white institution.

Evers' involvement with Negro rights began early as he organized movements and NAACP chapters, promoted voter registration, and urged economic boycotts. He became a member of NAACP in 1952 and joined the staff in 1954. After the murder of Negro youth Emmett Till in 1955, Evers undertook to gather evidence on the crime, going about the countryside dressed as a fieldhand.

Amid heightening tension and bitterness with white citizens' leaders, threats to the safety of his wife and children, and, eventually, a fire bomb thrown at his home, Evers continued a heavy schedule as NAACP secretary until 1963. On the night of June 12, he attended a mass rights rally at the New Jerusalem Baptist Church in Jackson, then drove to his home, arriving after two in the morning. As he got out of his car, he was hit in the back by a bullet from a high-powered rifle; he staggered to his doorway and collapsed. He died later that morning in a local hospital.

Fingerprints and other strong circumstantial evidence obtained by state and FBI officers led to the indictment for murder of Byron De La Beckwith, a white fertilizer salesman and amateur gun collector described by acquaintances as "obsessed with the racial issue." Two trials failed to bring in a verdict from the all-white Mississippi juries, and officials expressed doubt that there would ever be a third.

At a funeral attended by many white and Negro leaders, Medgar Evers was buried with military honors at Arlington Cemetery a week after his slaying.

James V. Forrestal
(1892–1949)

SECRETARY OF DEFENSE FORRESTAL's tragic death in 1949 shocked the nation and, in recalling the suicide of Ambassador John Winant, highlighted anew the question of health in top Government officers. The highest-ranking Government official ever to take his own life, this complex and driven man was diagnosed as suffering from involutional melancholia, a severe depression similar to the operational fatigue found in front-line cases during the war. Indeed, typifying his boundless determination to excel, he was described as "in the 'front lines' seven days a week for eight years, first fighting the war, and then struggling with the problems of reorganization and unification."

James Vincent Forrestal was born in Matteawan, New York, February 15, 1892, the third child and third son of John and Mary Forrestal. The father was an industrious immigrant from County Cork who become prosperous in construction and real estate and was active in state military and political affairs. Mary Forrestal was a strong-minded, devout woman, and wanted her son to become a priest; he severely disappointed both parents, however, by turning away from Catholicism in his teens and later marrying a divorced woman not of that faith.

Forrestal was a sickly child and, despite a lifelong preoccupation with sports, never achieved a robust physique. Though only five feet ten, and a hundred and fifty pounds, his carriage and address created an air of toughness and magnetism, and a broken nose acquired from athletic club boxing lent a pugnacious cachet to this impression.

In 1911 he enrolled at Dartmouth, but in 1912 transferred to Princeton, so he could "meet people who counted for something." Undeniably, the friendships formed there were helpful later on. He was a good student, became editor of the *Daily Princetonian*, then inexplicably left college without receiving a degree, six weeks before graduation in 1915, after having been voted "Most Likely to Succeed."

During World War I, Forrestal enlisted in the Navy in 1917, won naval aviator's wings, and after serving at various United States bases, resigned as a first lieutenant in 1919.

Young Forrestal had joined the influential New York investment firm of Dillon, Read and Company in 1916, and upon rejoining it after the war, his rise there was meteoric. His long hours and indefatigable dedication to business produced a series of financial coups that were the talk of the "Street" and led to his becoming a partner by 1923, vice-president by 1926, and in 1938, the president.

In 1926, he married Josephine Ogden, an editor of *Vogue*, but they never became very close and spent little time together during the last fifteen years of their marriage. They had two sons, with each of whom his relationship was that of "a Victorian father and his son."

Company connections were severed in 1940 when President Roosevelt named Forrestal an administrative assistant. Two months later he took over the newly created post of Undersecretary of the Navy, which he filled until he succeeded as forty-ninth Secretary of the Navy upon the death of

Frank Knox in 1944. Here he demonstrated the wide interpretation of his duties and unremitting drive that had characterized his business career. Tireless in promoting naval de-
partments and personnel, he originated the idea for the
Japanese surrender aboard the battleship *Missouri*.

In September, 1947, James Forrestal became the first
United States Secretary of Defense. He served with characteristic distinction amid constant controversy and trouble with
the press and business, congressional, and military leaders, his
troubles exacerbated by rapidly worsening health, until he
resigned in March, 1949. President Truman bestowed the
Distinguished Service Medal upon him for his outstanding
work. Shortly afterward, a very sick man, he was admitted for
psychiatric care to Bethesda Naval Hospital in Maryland, and
placed in a sixteenth-floor suite built for President Roosevelt.

During the early morning hours of May 22, 1949, after
copying out a passage from Sophocles' brooding "Chorus
From Ajax," Forrestal culminated several previous suicide
attempts by leaping to his death from a hall window. He was
buried with full military honors before an enormous crowd
at Arlington Cemetery.

Admiral William F. Halsey, Jr.
(1882–1959)

EARLY in 1942, when American fortunes of war against the Japanese in the Pacific were giving few people much cause for optimism, salty Vice Admiral "Bull" Halsey said, "Of course we're going to win the Solomons. Has there ever been any doubt about this?" He then proceeded to register against heavy odds what has been called the most smashing naval victory in World War II. Leading naval sea and air units in six simultaneous attacks on the Marshall and Gilbert Islands, Halsey, who "would rather be on time and wrong than late and right," caught the Japanese off guard, sank sixteen ships, shot down thirty-six planes, destroyed countless more in hangars, left fuel dumps in flaming wreckage. The spectacular raids brought him the Distinguished Service Medal and promotion to full admiral.

Headed for the Navy from the beginning by his parents, Annapolis graduate Captain William Frederick and Anna Halsey, William Frederick, Jr., was born in Elizabeth, New Jersey on October 30, 1882. He attended elementary and prep schools in California and Pennsylvania, the Naval Academy Preparatory School in Annapolis; entertained the idea of becoming a doctor, spending a year at the University of Virginia's medical school; and finally entered the United States Naval Academy in 1900. Then known as "Pudge," he was active both scholastically and athletically, played two years of football, and graduated in 1904, twenty-seventh in a class of 114.

Early in his career, Halsey saw duty aboard destroyers and during World War I served aboard patrol and escort vessels. Operating from a base in Ireland, the young officer won the Navy Cross for his valorous performance in mined, submarine-infested waters. Following the war, he served as naval attaché to United States embassies in Berlin, Christiania, Copenhagen and Stockholm.

In 1919, Lieutenant Halsey married Frances Gandy, of Norfolk, Virginia. They had two children, Margaret and William Frederick III.

Later he attended the army and navy war colleges, then underwent flight training, winning his wings in 1934 at the age of fifty-two, and subsequently headed the Pensacola air station. He rose to rear admiral in 1938, and took charge of a division of aircraft carriers.

With the outbreak of World War II, and after the Gilbert and Marshall Island forays, Halsey was given command over all United States Navy forces in the South Pacific in October, 1942. That November, he defeated the Japanese in a running battle through the waters of the Solomons. In June, 1943, he directed landing operations of marines and other personnel who captured New Georgia Island, and in November performed the same function at Bougainville, largest of the Solomon Islands, sinking five Japanese ships and damaging four in the action. This was the year in which Admiral Halsey was awarded the Congressional Medal of Honor.

His reputation now established as one of the Navy's most valuable combat officers, Halsey was named commander of the Third Fleet in June, 1944, and toward the end of October, in company with the Seventh Fleet, he supported General MacArthur's landings in the Philippines. They engaged the Japanese at Leyte Gulf, and in a week of fierce fighting, sank sixty enemy vessels of all sorts. Early the following year at the successful invasion of Luzon, largest of the Philippines, Halsey's forces shortstopped Japanese reinforcements so effectively that soon their ships scarcely ventured to leave their harbors.

Admiral Halsey's combat career was fittingly capped in 1945 when Japanese surrender ceremonies were held aboard his flagship, the battleship *Missouri*.

He was elevated to five-star rank in 1946, retired from active service the same year, then became vice-president for the Pacific service of Pan American Airways and president of International Telecommunication Laboratories. His war experiences appeared in the book *Admiral Halsey's Story* in 1947. He died August 16, 1959 at Fisher's Island, N.Y.

As one who disdained spit-and-polish, the stocky admiral, a naval cap tilted rakishly above his red, weatherbeaten face, often paced the bridge in carpet slippers to ease his aching feet. Very popular with his men, he was glad to overlook minor defects if the turrets gained a naval "E." He said of his rough-and-ready strategical approach, "I believe in violating rules. We violate them every day. We do the unexpected."

Chief Justice Oliver Wendell Holmes
(1841–1935)

CALLED by Justice Cardozo, "the greatest legal intellect in the history of the English-speaking judiciary," Oliver Wendell Holmes, Jr., sprang from a culture rich with New England and Puritan traditions and it helped shape his entire life and philosophy, though he himself was never religious nor parochial.

One of a family of two boys and a girl, Holmes was born in Boston, March 8, 1841. His father, with whom he was in subtly competitive conflict throughout his life, was Oliver Wendell Holmes, Sr., a witty, egotistic physician and prolific versifier and essayist; his maternal grandfather was an associate justice of the Massachusetts Supreme Court. A grandmother, Anne Bradstreet, was known in the American literary scene as the "Tenth Muse." As a boy, he vacationed at a family farm where he met such neighbors as Longfellow, Hawthorne and Melville. Emerson he also knew, and revered. After private school, with Cabot Lodge as a classmate, he entered Harvard at sixteen, but joined the Union Army as a private shortly before graduation in 1861.

Holmes went south as a second lieutenant of infantry with the 20th Massachusetts Regiment, part of the Army of the Potomac. He was a sturdy young officer and once, in company with Major Paul Revere, forced an enraged innkeeper at pistol point to empty twenty barrels of liquor into the street, to prevent recruits from getting drunk. Later, on another occasion during pitched battle, he spied a tall, stovepipe-hatted figure standing on a parapet where bullets were flying thickest, and yelled, "Get down, you fool!" President Lincoln got down, turned to Holmes, and said, "Captain, I am glad you know how to talk to civilians."

After three years of fighting, during which he had been breveted to lieutenant colonel, wounded in the chest at Ball's Bluff, in the neck at Antietam, and in the foot at Fredericksburg, Holmes was invalided out as a captain. Back in Boston, he found himself a hero, but, with his unromantic nature, was unimpressed and described war as "an organized bore." Nevertheless, it left a deep and lasting mark on his character and thought, his staunch patriotism, his belief in man's fulfilling a cosmic destiny larger than himself, like a larva, as he said, "preparing a chamber for the winged thing it never has seen but is to be."

Though leaning strongly to philosophy, in 1864 he entered Harvard to study law, with misgivings that lasted for years. Upon finishing in 1866, he took the first of many trips to England where he made friends with Gladstone, John Stuart Mill, Benjamin Jowett and other prominent thinkers, who were charmed by his wit and intellect.

Holmes began law practice in Boston in 1867, throwing himself into feverish study and mastering all areas of law and its interpretation. He lectured at Harvard and edited the *American Law Review* from 1870 to 1873. In 1881 he published *The Common Law*, with its famous opening words, "The life of the law has not been logic, it has been experience." It was a work of seminal scholarship causing a broad reorientation of juridical inquiry. It immediately became, and remains today, a fundamental part of American legal thought. The great response it elicited among legal circles led to the creation of a chair for him at Harvard, and later to an appointment to the bench of the Massachusetts Supreme Court to which he ascended in 1883.

Miss Fanny Bowditch Dixwell became his bride in 1872. She was lively and charming, with an original and perceptive mind which had a strong and salutory effect upon his life and career. Once when, as was his habit, he was ranting and cussing about the house over something, she left him a note on the mantelpiece reading, "During my life I have been beset by many troubles, most of which never happened." Holmes found it, roared with laughter, and quoted it often afterwards. When she died in 1929, he said to a friend, "For sixty years she made life poetry for me."

For twenty years Holmes remained at the Massachusetts supreme court, becoming its chief justice in 1899, and writing fifty volumes of opinion. President Theodore Roosevelt appointed him to the United States Supreme Court in 1902, where he later became known as the "Great Dissenter" because of his trenchant dissenting opinions, which, though relatively few in number, changed the very fabric of law. His erudition was vast, and his decisions were characterized by an almost cavalier brevity and illuminative insight.

Justice Holmes was a tall man, six feet four, with keen eyes under imposing brows, sweeping, grandee mustaches, and a full head of white hair. His marvelous physique carried him through a major operation late in life and his faculties never became impaired despite his great age. Indeed, some of his most powerful decisions were written during his ninth decade.

At the age of eighty-eight he became Chief Justice, upon

the death of William Howard Taft, but his strength was failing, and four years later he submitted his resignation in his own beautiful script, beginning, "The time has come and I bow to the inevitable."

He died March 6, 1935, and was buried with full military honors next to his wife in Arlington Cemetery. President Franklin Roosevelt subsequently delivered a eulogy in a message to Congress.

With no accompanying comment Justice Holmes left the bulk of his substantial personal estate to the nation after his death. It was the largest unrestricted gift ever given. Fittingly, the money was used to finance a history of the Supreme Court.

General Philip Kearny
(1814–1862)

As one of the most mercurial and tempestuous figures in American military history, it was appropriate for Philip Kearny to be born June 1, 1814, on New York's lower Broadway, at the height of a fearsome torrential rainstorm. His father, Philip Kearny, was a wine and liquor broker of wealth and distinguished social position. An only child, young Philip spent a great deal of time with his fond maternal grandfather, after his mother's death in 1823.

Upon finishing private schooling, he entered Columbia University in 1830, when family opposition thwarted his desire to enroll at West Point. His grandfather, who had lost all his sons, offered him $1,500 a year to pursue the ministry, but he rejected the offer and studied law, graduating with honors in 1834. He immediately made a trip to Europe, where he devoted most of his attention to various military maneuvers.

In 1836, Grandfather Watts died, leaving young Kearny an inheritance of a million dollars. Fond of horses, and a fearless rider from boyhood, he at once applied for a cavalry commission and received his second lieutenancy in 1837. This was smoothed by an old friend, General Winfield Scott, whom he had met as a boy through his uncle, Major Stephen Kearny, on visits to West Point when the general was commandant there.

He saw two years of service on the frontier at Fort Leavenworth, Kansas, with the 1st United States Dragoons, commanded by his uncle, before being assigned in 1839 to the
French Royal Cavalry School at Saumur.

His dashing performance' with the Chasseurs d'Afrique
during the Algerian engagements in 1840 won him the Légion d'Honneur and the sobriquet "Kearny *le magnifique*."
He returned home to become aide-de-camp to Army Commander in Chief General Macomb and to his successor, General Scott. "Old Fuss 'n' Feathers" Scott was a high-tempered
man, as was Kearny, and their relationship was marked by
considerable friction. Kearny's marriage in 1841 to Diana
Bullitt, a descendant of Revolutionary War hero George
Rogers Clark, and Captain William Clark of expeditionary
fame, was at best a stormy one. Although it produced five
children, it ended in divorce in 1858. That same year,
Kearny remarried and had one child, an adored son, who
died two years later on Washington's Birthday.

With the outbreak of the Mexican War in 1846, Kearny
who had resigned his commission only a month earlier, was
reinstated to act as General Scott's bodyguard in the advance
on the City of Mexico. While raising and resplendently
outfitting a company chiefly at his own expense, he established recruiting headquarters in Springfield, Illinois, and
was aided in his efforts to buy matched gray horses by a local
lawyer named Lincoln. Later, leading a charge at Churu-
busco, his left arm was shattered. As the arm was amputated,
his head was held firmly by General Franklin Pierce, later
President. Promoted to major for his courage under fire, he
saw further service until 1851 when he retired to improve his
hundred-acre estate, "Bellegrave" (modeled after a fifteenth-
century castle in France near Saumur), near Newark, New
Jersey, in the section now called Kearny.

Retirement did not last long, and in 1859 he returned to France as attaché to the staff of General Morris, commander of cavalry of the Imperial Guard of Napoleon III. Kearny engaged in every cavalry charge at Magenta and Solferino, where his conduct won him a second Légion d'Honneur, the only time a foreigner had been so decorated.

With the outbreak of the Civil War he hastened from his home in Paris to America, where as a brigadier general in command of the 1st New Jersey Brigade, he participated in at least twelve engagements, including the second Battle of Bull Run, first with McClellan's Army of the Potomac, then under Pope as a major general. His dash and spirit moved E. C. Stedman to commemorate him in the poem "Kearny at Seven Pines."

On the stormy night of September 1, 1862, following his custom of riding through the country learning the roads around a new position, he unwittingly entered enemy lines near Chantilly, Virginia, and was shot dead by a single bullet fired during a flash of lightning, thus leaving life as he had entered it.

General Robert E. Lee, who had known Kearny during the Mexican War, forwarded the body to General Pope under a flag of truce; later, at the request of Kearny's widow, he sent Kearny's horse, saddle and sword.

It was precisely the manner in which Kearny wished to die. With *"Dolce et decorum pro patria more"* as his motto, he once wrote his wife, "I shall ride out gaily to meet my fate, with the cacophony of battle ringing in my ears." Ride gaily he always did; spurring forward, his képi cocked at an angle, the reins in his teeth, his empty left sleeve was flying out behind him and his right arm was brandishing a flashing saber when he fell.

John Fitzgerald Kennedy
(1917–1963)

IT has become commonplace to treat the story of our thirty-fifth President as a tableau of incredible legend . . . born to fabulous wealth and possessed of princely charm and hand-someness, he accompanied his Croesus of a father on state visits to the courts of kings, performed wartime feats of chivalric valor, married a highborn lady as comely and dec-orous as a fairy tale princess, stoically endured epic scourges of physical pain and the deaths of a son, a brother, and a sister; picked up the banner of his fallen brother and gal-lantly carried it to storybook heights of power and réclame . . . and then perished before his time in a Gothic tale of blood and violence. The Kennedy mythology, however, is all hard fact.

As one of the nine children of millionaire Joseph Kennedy and his wife Rose, he was born May 29, 1917, at Brookline, Massachusetts, and christened John Fitzgerald after his ma-ternal grandfather, the colorful "Honey Fitz," onetime mayor of Boston. Like all the Kennedy children, John re-ceived a million-dollar trust fund from his father. Frequent illnesses did not prevent him from being active and ener-getic, then or later. He went to Choate School and vacationed in Europe before studying under Harold Laski at the Lon-don School of Economics during 1935–36. He then entered

Harvard and was graduated with honors in 1940. He combined scholarship with the keen Kennedy eye for economics. His political science thesis became the best-selling book *Why England Slept,* with his analysis of the reasons for England's unpreparedness for World War II using ideas gained in prewar Britain while his father was ambassador to the Court of St. James.

The book reflected the Jack Kennedy who later worked briefly as a journalist, who liked to write and thought of himself as something of a writer, who was deft and often poetic in his public utterances, and who wrote *Profiles In Courage,* a best-seller that won the Pulitzer Prize for biography in 1957.

When World War II came, Kennedy entered the Navy, and wound up in the Solomon Islands, a stringy, cocky young lieutenant in command of a PT boat. During a night run, his boat was rammed and cut in two by a Japanese destroyer. Thrown into the water with a badly and permanently injured back, he swam for fifteen hours, towing one injured man and guiding and exhorting the other members of his crew to the safety of an island. Later, the highly publicized episode won him the Navy and Marine Corps Medal.

Elder brother Joe, a pilot in the European Theatre of Operations, was killed in action and his far-reaching political ambitions fell to Jack to fulfill as a clan responsibility. Beginning in 1946, he won three terms to Congress as Democratic representative from Massachusetts' 11th District, piling up tremendous electoral majorities in each. In 1952, he wrested election to the Senate from incumbent Henry Cabot Lodge . . . a victory made sweeter by the fact that in 1916 the same fight had been waged by their grandfathers . . .

but in that one old Henry Cabot Lodge had whipped John "Honey Fitz" Fitzgerald.

The following year, Senator Kennedy married Jacqueline Bouvier, a beautiful and cultured product of Vassar and the Sorbonne. Though they lost children to miscarriage and death in infancy, they had two children, Caroline and John F., Jr.

Reelected in 1956, Senator Kennedy set about seeking his party's Vice-Presidential nomination, but fortunately for his political plans, lost it to Senator Estes Kefauver, who, along with Presidential nominee Adlai Stevenson, was swept away in the Republican tide that year.

During his fourteen years in Congress, Kennedy's political thinking and voting record defied classification. He joined the moderate liberals of both parties but hewed to no predictable political line. Although he was never admitted to the powerful "inner circle" of Senate potentates he was later chosen to sit on the important Foreign Relations Committee.

In campaigns characterized by hustle and shrewdness, and a consuming love for the infighting of rough-and-tumble politics, he first sought the Democratic Presidential nomination in 1960 and won it on the first ballot. He then defeated Republican Vice-President Richard Nixon by one of the narrowest margins in United States history. Called "the first Irish Brahmin," Kennedy was the first man born in the twentieth century and the first Roman Catholic to be elected President.

Also the youngest President ever elected, John Kennedy brought youth, attractiveness, and vigor to the White House, in himself, his family, and his aides. Undeniably a charismatic leader, he endowed his office with grace and the new

Government with excitement. But an evaluation of his record must always be one of promise and conjecture.

On November 22, 1963, he arrived in Dallas to make a speech. Sitting in an open limousine as part of a motorcade, he was shot and killed by high-calibre rifle bullets fired from ambush. He collapsed in Jackie's lap and was sped to a hospital where he was pronounced dead. Lee Harvey Oswald was arrested and charged with the assassination. Evidence conclusively supported the indictment, though he denied any guilt. A few days later, the indictment became academic, when Oswald, still in custody, was shot and killed with a revolver, by Jack Ruby, who professed to be crazed with grief over President Kennedy's death. Vice-President Lyndon Johnson succeeded to the Presidency.

At solemn ceremonies attended by heads of state from all over the world, and thousands of mourners, President Kennedy was buried in Arlington Cemetery on a slope beneath the Lee Mansion. An "Eternal Flame" was installed at his grave, resembling the one commemorating the Unknown Soldier at the Arc de Triomphe, in Paris.

Admiral William D. Leahy
(1875–1959)

IN 1939, with militant thunderheads piling up over Europe, Admiral Leahy was retired at the statutory age of sixty-four. President Roosevelt pinned a Distinguished Service Medal on him and said, "Bill, if we have a war, you're going to be right back here helping me run it." We did and he was. The redoubtable Leahy proceeded to cap a salty, forty-six year career, of which twenty-two years were spent at sea, with a second career as governor of Puerto Rico, ambassador to the Vichy French puppet Government, and chief of staff for Presidents Roosevelt and Truman.

A native Iowan, William Daniel Leahy was born in the small town of Hampton on May 6, 1875, the son of Michael and Rose Hamilton Leahy. After finishing high school in Ashland, Wisconsin, he entered Annapolis and was graduated in 1897. He passed midshipman on the battleship *Oregon* and was aboard when she made her spectacular dash from the United States Pacific coast around Cape Horn to Cuba. With guns blazing, she joined the fleet in time for the Battle of Santiago Harbor, July 3, 1898, and helped annihilate Admiral Cervera's Spanish armada. By 1916, after seeing lively action in the Philippine Insurrection, the Boxer Rebellion, the Nicaraguan Occupation and the Haitian Campaign, he was commander of the USS *Dolphin* during the Mexican punitive expedition. It was at this time that he became friends with an occasional guest aboard his vessel, Assistant Secretary of the Navy Franklin D. Roosevelt.

In 1904 he married the attractive Louise Tenet Harrington of San Francisco. Their only child was a son who followed his father's footsteps into the Navy and became a respected flag rank officer in his own right.

During World War I Leahy won the Navy Cross for his outstanding services in ferrying troops through the German submarine packs in the North Atlantic.

Though it took him twenty-seven years to reach his captaincy, he rose rapidly thereafter. Between World Wars I and II he served successively as chief of the Naval Bureau of Ordnance, chief of the Bureau of Navigation and finally chief of the Bureau of Naval Operations until his retirement in 1939. Leahy was the only man in naval history to have been chief of both the important bureaus of Ordnance and Operations.

Prior to our own entrance into World War II, Leahy was appointed ambassador to the Vichy Government in France after the ailing General Pershing was forced to turn down the assignment. Although never a diplomat, Leahy served well in the highly delicate position of America's forward diplomatic observer of the Nazi regime.

He became President Roosevelt's wartime chief of staff in 1942. He accompanied FDR to the historic confrontations between Roosevelt and the other allied leaders. He was the senior advisor at the bitterly controversial Yalta conference. With the new rank of a five-star admiral of the fleet, awarded in 1944, Leahy stayed on as chief of staff under President Truman.

His second retirement came in 1949, accompanied by a

second, well-deserved Distinguished Service Medal. The following year he published an account of his Washington experiences, the popular *I Was There*.

The tall, weatherbeaten, bushy-browed fleet admiral was strict, and at times his tongue could be rough as a cob. He once criticized slave labor in Russia so outspokenly that the Soviets demanded an official apology. He was known as a strong "Big Navy" man, and dismissed the atom bomb as "a lot of hooey," contemptuously ranking it somewhere with poison gas and bacteriological warfare. Said to be an "open-minded conservative," he was generally regarded as a straightforward, but hard-headed, businesslike personality. Off-duty, he was easy and friendly, fond of relaxing at golf and bridge and playing with his grandchildren.

On April 30, 1959, Admiral Leahy entered Bethesda Naval Hospital in Maryland, and several weeks later, stricken with a cerebro-vascular disorder, he died on July 20th, with his son at his bedside.

Major Pierre Charles L'Enfant
(1754–1825)

It took the "Forgotten Architect" ten years to collect his modest fee for designing the city of Washington, D.C. In September, 1789, Pierre L'Enfant submitted an application to President Washington to design a "Seat of Government," in a letter containing the sensible and prophetic words "The plan should be drawn on such a scale as to leave room for that aggrandizement and embellishment which the increase of the wealth of the nation will permit it to pursue, at any period however remote." After some contention, the "L'Enfant Plan" was accepted in December, 1791. Washington suggested a fee of $2500 to $3000, but L'Enfant quietly refused and said little more until the death of "his general." Succeeding years were spent in attempts to collect for his work, and finally in 1810, a dilatory Congress awarded him $666.67, with interest, making a total of $1394.20. Virtually all of this was claimed by creditors.

Pierre L'Enfant's life began in comfortable circumstances. He was born in Paris, August 2, 1754, another in a family line of artists, to a father of the same name who was "Painter in Ordinary" to the King and director of the Gobelin tapestry factory. His mother was Marie Charlotte Leullier, daughter of a royal court officer. As a young man he studied under his father at the Academie Royale de Peinture et de

Sculpture, and acquired his knowledge of architecture while studying engineering, of which architecture was considered a branch in those days.

He was one of the first to offer his services to the American Revolution, and, as a newly-commissioned second lieutenant in the French Colonial Troops, he sailed from France early in 1777 on a ship laden with arms and supplies for the revolutionaries. Upon his arrival he became an aide to General von Steuben, with headquarters near Lafayette. He wintered at Valley Forge in 1777–78 and whiled away dreary hours with his clever pencil, once producing a likeness of Washington for Lafayette. He became known as the "Artist of the Revolution" and it is believed that he designed the badge for the wounded, today's Purple Heart. A specialty of his was the construction of forts.

Congress promoted him to captain in 1778 and in the autumn of 1779 he fought with General Pulaski at the Siege of Savannah. In the same battle in which the general was killed, L'Enfant was severely wounded and hospitalized in Charleston, South Carolina. The British captured that city in 1780 and he was made a prisoner of war, but was soon exchanged and moved north, where he became a member of Washington's staff. In May, 1783, he was breveted to major.

At the war's end, L'Enfant went to Paris, but returned to the United States in 1785, acting as interpreter for the French sculptor Houdon, who was commissioned to do a statue of Washington at Mount Vernon. He subsequently became a fashionable bachelor architect in New York, living in style on lower Broadway, and he received the commission to restore Federal Hall for the first Congress of the United States and the inauguration of President Washington on

April 30, 1789. He also restored St. Paul's Chapel in New York and designed furniture for Duncan Phyfe.

Though later financial difficulties reduced him to near poverty, in 1812 he coolly declined an appointment as professor of engineering at West Point, despite urging by Secretary of State Monroe to accept. That same year, however, he did accept the commission to fortify Fort Washington, opposite Mount Vernon.

Pierre L'Enfant died June 14, 1825, still a bachelor, leaving an estate of $45. He was buried in a family plot at Chillum, Virginia, but a Congressional act in 1909 had him transferred to Arlington with military honors. In 1911, a monument was erected at his grave site, a table stone bearing an inscription of the "L'Enfant Plan" of the city of Washington, which his tomb overlooks.

Robert Todd Lincoln
(1843–1926)

ROBERT LINCOLN sometimes observed sadly that not many other men had been near at hand for the murder of three American Presidents. He had kept an all-night vigil at the bedside of his dying father, Abraham Lincoln. (It is one of history's more curious coincidences that on an earlier occasion he himself had been saved from falling off a moving train by the hand of Edwin, brother of Abraham Lincoln's assassin, John Wilkes Booth.) He had been one of the crowd of well-wishers at the Washington railroad station who saw President Garfield shot by Guiteau. And, twenty years later, at the Buffalo Pan-American Exposition, he was nearby when Czolgosz shot President McKinley. He once curtly refused an invitation to a Presidential affair with "No, I'm not going, and they'd better not ask me, because there is a certain fatality about Presidential functions when I am present."

Born August 1, 1843, at the Globe Tavern, a boarding-house in Springfield, Illinois, he was the eldest and only survivor among the four sons of Abraham and Mary Todd Lincoln. Reserved, aloof, never quite part of the family circle, the precocious boy seemed to be molded after the more aristocratic Todd family. He was given every educational advantage that his father was conscious of having missed and was sent to Harvard in 1859. Springfield schools being what they were, he failed fifteen of the sixteen subjects in the entrance examinations, and then spent a preparatory year at Exeter Academy in New Hampshire before being accepted. His letter of introduction to Harvard's president from Stephen A. Douglas characterized young Bob as the son of his friend "with whom I have lately been canvassing the state of Illinois."

Amid the adverse criticism that was to surround him sporadically throughout his life, Lincoln was kept in school by his father through the insistence of his morbidly protective mother, while his associates were entering the Union Army. After his graduation in 1864 and four months at Harvard Law School, his father secured a commission for him as captain on General Grant's staff, after he had reportedly enlisted as a private. He was present during the Confederate surrender at Appomattox Courthouse, but then, as always later, wishing to avoid the appearance of capitalizing on his name, he stood outside on the porch where he "could not even hear General Lee's voice." He never had his picture taken while wearing his uniform.

Robert Lincoln later studied law in Chicago and began practice there in 1867. A year later, after several years' courtship, he married Mary, daughter of Senator Harlan of Iowa. He was an exceptionally devoted husband and father, and two daughters survived him, while his son's death in childhood precluded perpetuation of the Lincoln name. A good businessman, he soon gained a profitable clientele among the great railroad and corporate interests with which he was always identified and which ultimately made him a millionaire.

During the years of his increasingly successful business and legal activities, Lincoln, as a staunch conservative Republican, maintained a mild interest in politics and was repeatedly mentioned as a candidate for high elective office by politicians not averse to coining political currency from his name, but he always declined. In 1881, however, he reluctantly accepted Garfield's appointing him Secretary of War and spent an uneventful tenure until 1885. Four years later, to his surprise and dismay, President Harrison named him minister to England (the last envoy to the Court of St. James with the rank of minister, all later ones being elevated to the rank of ambassador).

His return to America saw him immersed in corporation work as before, until 1897 when his long-time representation of the Pullman Company led to his assuming first its presidency and then its chairmanship. During the great Pullman strike of 1894, he had been the subject of bitter criticism comparing him unfavorably with his father for his seeming lack of sympathy for the working man but, though normally thin-skinned, he ignored it.

Poor health forced him to retire to Washington in 1912, and he spent summers at his princely "Hildene" in Manchester, Vermont. His near-total seclusion in Vermont was spent making astronomical observations and solving algebraic problems. He spoke of "sliding downhill gently" and lived the quiet life of a recluse until he died in his sleep at "Hildene" on June 26, 1926.

A full-fleshed man of middle height, bearded and bespectacled, Robert Lincoln was as impeccable in his social relations as he was in his grooming, and he spent the better part of his life zealously protecting the family name from sensation-seekers, detractors, and the merely curious. By his own admission, the most cruel pain he ever suffered was the public humiliation brought about by his mother's protracted display of irrational behavior following the assassination, and his being forced at last to commit her to a mental institution. His delicacy prompted him to destroy some of his father's papers and to deposit the remainder in the Library of Congress, with instructions that they remain sealed until twenty-one years after his own death. As for being the bearer of a great name, he expressed his feelings when he remarked late in life, concerning his appointments as Secretary of War, minister to England, and chairman of the Pullman Company, "They never wanted me; they wanted the son of the President."

General George C. Marshall

(1880–1959)

To the chagrin of publishers everywhere, the retired General Marshall steadfastly refused to write his memoirs. He was once visited by a senior editor of one of the major publishing houses. After some plain and fancy pleading, the frustrated editor finally said, "But, General, we are offering you one million dollars."

"My dear sir," said the old soldier gravely, "I am not interested in one million dollars."

If he had been, there would have been much to tell of a long and brilliant career that began in Uniontown, Pennsylvania, where he was born, New Year's Eve, 1880. His father was the prosperous fuel merchant George Catlett Marshall, Sr., and his mother, the former Laura Bradford. Young Marshall entered Virginia Military Institute in 1897 and distinguished himself there by winning all-Southern honors as tackle on the football team, by refusing to inform on upperclassmen who seriously wounded him with a bayonet during hazing rituals, and by becoming first captain of the cadet corps in his senior year.

After graduation in 1901, he went into the Army and first saw duty in the Philippines and at posts in the western United States. He graduated from the United States Infantry-Cavalry School in 1907 and the Army Staff College in 1908 and later taught at the latter for two years. Once again in the Philippines, during 1913–16, he served the last year as aide to General Liggett and drew from General Franklin Bell the enthusiastic endorsement, "greatest military genius since Stonewall Jackson."

Upon United States entry into World War I, Marshall was sent to France, where he was assigned to GHQ. He requested a direct combat command, but his rare talents as a staff officer were too well recognized and highly prized, and he was refused. For his superb direction of the successful Saint-Mihiel and Meuse-Argonne offensives, he was elevated to temporary lieutenant colonel from his recently won captaincy. General Pershing tabbed him as aide from 1919 to 1920.

In 1924, the lieutenant colonelcy now permanent, he was sent with the infantry to Tientsin for three years, followed by a year's instructorship at the Army War College and then assignment as assistant commander of the Infantry School at Fort Benning, Georgia, from 1928 to 1932. He was made brigadier general in 1936 and was appointed assistant chief of staff in 1938. A year later, with war threatening, he moved to chief of staff with the rank of full general.

Reading the signs correctly, General Marshall insisted upon peacetime conscription and calling up reserves and the National Guard. After Pearl Harbor, he became chief strategist for the Allied powers and directed operations in both the European and Pacific theatres. In 1944, he was promoted to the rank of five-star general of the Army, a title created especially for him in deference to his assertion that he "did not care to be called Marshal Marshall." By war's end, he had raised the army from a puny body of 200,000 to a force of over eight million.

Within a week after resigning his wartime post, he was sent in November, 1945, as President Truman's personal envoy with the rank of ambassador to China to try to resolve differences between Communists and Nationalists. The year he spent there effected little more than an uneasy cease-fire.

President Truman recalled him in January, 1947, for a new job, and he became the first professional soldier ever to be appointed Secretary of State. At the Harvard Commencement in June of that year, he outlined the Truman Doctrine, plans for direct economic assistance to war-stricken Europe. Eventually extending twelve and a half billion dollars to sixteen European nations, it became known as the Marshall Plan, and won him the Nobel Peace Prize in 1953.

Following major surgery in the previous year, Marshall resigned as Secretary of State in 1949 and was succeeded by Dean Acheson. He served briefly as president of the Red Cross, then as Secretary of Defense from 1950 to 1951, during the Korean War. He at last retired to live quietly on his estate near Pinehurst, North Carolina. In March of 1959, after suffering a stroke at home, he entered Walter Reed Hospital in Washington. While there he was visited by former President Truman, and Winston Churchill in company with President Eisenhower, a former protégé. He died October 16, 1959.

General Marshall was tall, serious, aristocratic, soldierly in all respects. No legends grew up about him. Far from having a nickname—no one even presumed to call him "George." There was long-standing ill feeling between him and General MacArthur, though it was characteristic of his integrity that he later urged award of the Congressional Medal of Honor for MacArthur's World War II Manila fighting. He was keen to command the Normandy invasion, but when President

Roosevelt told him he "wouldn't sleep nights if you were out of the country," once again he stayed behind to staff operations.

In addition to his being a Nobel laureate, the general received honorary doctorates from Columbia, Princeton, Harvard, Oxford, and nearly a dozen other universities, was decorated with the Distinguished Service Medal, Silver Star, Order of the Bath, Croix de Guerre, Légion d'Honneur, and orders from Montenegro, Italy, Panama, Brazil, Ecuador, Peru, Morocco, Cuba, Chile and Russia.

Admiral Marc Mitscher
(1887–1947)

As commander of the Navy's massive and deadly fast carrier Task Force 58 against the Japanese in World War II, his code name was "Bald Eagle." Admiral Mitscher was bald, struck fiercely from the air, and was an utterly fearless and tenacious fighter. He was, on the other hand, known familiarly to his men as "Uncle Pete," but with his little leathery body, wizened face, and spectacles perched halfway down his nose under piercing blue eyes and bushy ginger eyebrows, he was, indeed, the bald eagle of the Pacific.

This colorful but taciturn and modest man of contrasts was born Marc Andrew Mitscher on January 26, 1887. The second of three children of German immigrants Oscar and Myrta Mitscher, his birthplace was Hillsborough, Wisconsin. The family soon moved to Oklahoma Territory where Oscar became Oklahoma City's second mayor. Young Marc was educated in Washington D.C., where he wintered with family friends.

In June, 1904, a congressional friend of his father's gained Mitscher an appointment to the United States Naval Academy, where he was a "wooden" student, occupying the foot of the class from the beginning. The independent plebe soon amassed 280 demerits against an allowable 250.

He was "bilged out" after two years over a hazing incident

but won reinstatement, only to begin all over again, and he proceeded to rack up 100 demerits in twenty-four hours.

He graduated in 1910, and after sea duty assignments, married Frances Smalley in 1913. They were a devoted couple, and after the early loss of a baby, had no children. In his domestic life he was so gentle that his perplexed bride could scarcely credit later stories of his lively involvement in several street and barroom brawls. Though a salty aviator himself and unscathed survivor of many crashes, the admiral would not allow his wife to fly until 1944.

He himself reported in 1915 as one of the thirteen original students for flight training with the rickety, embryonic Naval Air Force at Pensacola, Florida. He won his wings in 1916 and saw World War I service as aviation officer on Atlantic convoy duty. In 1918, he was placed in charge of the Miami Naval Air station.

Mitscher was detached to the historic Transatlantic Flight Division as pilot of one of three planes attempting man's first transatlantic flight in 1919. One plane made it, but Mitscher was forced down in shark-infested waters. Fished out of the Atlantic, he was taken to London, and feted by the Prince of Wales and the then Minister of War, Winston Churchill. He received the Navy Cross for his part, and later won many other decorations, among them two more Navy Crosses, two Distinguished Service Medals, the Legion of Merit, the Order of the Bath, and the Croix de Guerre. He was always quick and generous in bestowing decorations upon his men and pioneered in intraservice awards.

Succeeding years saw him active at the new Bureau of Naval Aeronautics and various other posts, always heavily engaged in the running military controversy between surface craft and air power adherents.

In 1941, as a Captain, he was given command of the aircraft carrier *Hornet*, the famed "Shangri-La" from which Colonel Doolittle's B-25's made the first bombing attacks on Tokyo in early 1942. Following the raid, Mitscher was made rear admiral and took part in the historic battle of Midway.

He spent a short tour of shore duty in Hawaii, then was sent to the beleaguered Guadalcanal to take on the rough, dirty, and dangerous job of commanding all allied aircraft in the Solomons. In 1943, General Twining, later Air Force chief of staff, relieved Mitscher of this post, which, he later admitted, was his toughest assignment. Mitscher returned to the United States a malarial wraith of 115 pounds.

After a few recuperative months on administrative duty in San Diego, he returned to Pearl Harbor in 1944 as commander of Task Force 58, with Captain Arleigh Burke as his chief of staff. Wearing his trademark long-billed cap and then nonregulation brown shoes, perched on the bridge of his flagship in a high swivel chair always facing aft ("to keep the wind out of my face"), Mitscher roamed the Pacific making lightning raids against the hated "yellowtails" at Truk, Guam, Iwo Jima and Ie Jima, where his friend the great war correspondent Ernie Pyle was killed. At the "Marianas Turkey Shoot," his forces shot down 346 enemy planes in one day, and at the Battle of Leyte Gulf, he played a major part in decisively smashing Japanese sea power. Finally, after having two ships shot out from under him, Mitscher saw his last action during the wild and bloody Okinawa campaign.

Returning to the United States in 1945, he became deputy chief of Naval Operations for Air; then, in 1946, the first aviator to receive fleet command, he was named to head the 8th Fleet, with headquarters at Norfolk.

While there, Mitscher, then a full four-star admiral, entered the base hospital, suffering from a recurrent heart ailment. He died in his sleep a few days after his sixtieth birthday, in the early morning hours of February 3, 1947, and was buried with a seventeen-gun salute in Arlington Cemetery, on the eastern slope below the Custis-Lee Mansion.

Admiral Robert Peary

(1856–1920)

In the sixty-below-zero Arctic winter night of 1898, Robert Peary set out upon his first attempt to reach the North Pole. During the grueling trek, he noted in his diary, "a suspicious 'wooden' feeling in the right foot led me to have my kamiks pulled off, and I found, to my annoyance, that both feet were frosted." He was then confined to camp for six weeks, but, though suffering great pain, discomfort and disappointment, he scratched on the cabin wall above his bunk the quotation from Seneca which was his lifelong motto, *Inveniam viam aut faciam*, "I shall find a way or make one." Following a dogsled trip across 250 miles of ice fields to his ship, Peary's toes were amputated, and he carried out all his subsequent explorations on makeshift stumps of feet.

Not long after Peary's birth on May 6, 1856, in Cresson, Pennsylvania, his father died, and the boy and his mother resettled in South Portland, Maine. There he spent a boyhood complete with everything but money, becoming an all-around sportsman and developing the passion for the out-of-doors that was to shape his career. He won a scholarship to Bowdoin College and graduated Phi Beta Kappa as a top student in civil engineering. He then worked for a short time with the United States Geodetic Survey, and in 1880 he entered the Civil Engineering Corps of the United States

Navy and was sent to Nicaragua on exploratory work in connection with the proposed Panama Canal.

By 1886, his long-time fascination with the North had crystallized with his being able to finance a small expedition to Greenland, then largely unknown. The limited results were unspectacular, but the trip gave Peary valuable experience and strengthened his resolve to reach the Pole.

In 1888 he married Josephine Diebitsch. Theirs was a happy if austere marriage. She became the first American woman to winter in the Arctic when, on the next Greenland expedition, in 1891, she accompanied him, along with Dr. Frederick A. Cook going as surgeon on his first Arctic trip, and the loyal and able Matt Henson, Peary's Negro personal assistant. Peary directed landing operations with both legs broken in a ship mishap. Later he went on to discover Independence Bay, man's northernmost point thus far. Twenty years later, explorers Knud Rasmussen and Peter Freuchen found the party's records cairn at the bay and noted that their footprints were still visible in the gravel around it.

Upon his return to America, Peary was acclaimed a hero and immediately set about financing a further expedition, largely through a lecture tour, during which he spoke 165 times in 100 days.

He sailed again in 1893, accompanied by a fourteen-man crew and the courageous, and now pregnant, Mrs. Peary. On her return trip three months later, she gave birth to a daughter, nicknamed "Snow Baby." This expedition yielded discovery of three huge meteorites, one of them the world's largest, currently displayed at the Hayden Planetarium.

He became a leading figure in the "Race for the Pole" an

event which held the turn-of-the-century world spellbound. The polar exploration became a race because the Danish explorer Sverdrup, contrary to traditions of exploration, had announced intentions of seeking the Pole, after Peary had made his own plans public. After countless delays of all sorts, Peary made his first serious attempt to reach the Pole in 1902, but all the trip produced of interest was his discovery of a species of caribou, which was named after him.

Another attempt was made in 1905, during which, in failing to reach their goal after incredible hardships, Peary and Henson nearly starved to death.

In July, 1908, Peary and his crew sailed from New York in his ship *Roosevelt*. Arriving at the assault site, he worked out a meticulously planned operation, set up five support camps stretching north, then began the final dash on February 28, 1909, in company with Henson and four Eskimo helpers. At last, on April 6, 1909, after twenty-three years of trying, Peary reached the North Pole.

Upon his return to Labrador in September, Peary found that his erstwhile assistant, Dr. Cook, had just returned from an expedition of his own and claimed to have reached the Pole first. The claim was prematurely accepted, but records offered in evidence showed that Cook (who later served a prison term for mail fraud) had perpetrated a hoax. After a protracted period of vitriolic debate, the long-suffering Peary's achievement was officially and generally recognized as authentic. His feat eventually brought him twenty-six medals and trophies and four honorary degrees.

After this last expedition, Peary was advanced to the rank of rear admiral and placed on the retired list. He continued a heavy schedule of lectures and activities with the Explorers'

Club, despite medical warnings that he was suffering from pernicious anemia. He died of the disease February 26, 1920, and was buried in Arlington Cemetery. Over his grave stands a granite sphere of the earth with a bronze star at the North Pole and engraved with the words of his motto.

General John J. Pershing
(1860–1948)

DURING World War I, in one of the many acrimonious conferences held by the Allies' Supreme War Council, a livid "Black Jack" Pershing rose to his feet and faced his fellow members, Clemençeau, Lloyd George and Orlando. Smashing his fist upon the table, he said, "Gentlemen, I have thought this thing over very deliberately, and I will not be coerced." The scene was characteristic of the situation and of the grim man who had undertaken to build an army out of nothing.

John Joseph Pershing's life was beset by conflict and difficulty from the beginning. He was born near Laclede, Missouri, September 13, 1860, to poor parents, John F. and Ann Thompson Pershing. While still in his teens, he taught country school to earn money for study at Kirksville Normal School. Through competitive examination, he won entry to West Point and graduated in 1886, thirtieth in a class of seventy-seven, after being president of his class and achieving the highest cadet rank of first captain.

The young lieutenant first saw action against the Apaches in Arizona, then was sent in 1890 in charge of scouts against the Sioux in the Dakotas, where he took part in the Battle of Wounded Knee. He became military instructor at the University of Nebraska and acquired a law degree there in 1893 before transferring to West Point as tactics instructor. He fought in the Spanish-American War, his conduct earning him a Silver Star and the accolade from his commander, "Pershing is the coolest man under fire I ever saw."

Shortly afterward, Pershing organized and headed the Bureau of Insular Affairs, then was sent to the Philippines to pacify the fierce Moros of Mindanao. He accomplished that bloody job by 1903. He went in 1905 to Tokyo as military attaché and observed the Manchurian campaign with Kuroki's army.

President Theodore Roosevelt rewarded Captain Pershing for his Philippine service by promoting him straight to brigadier general in 1906. The unusual step jumped him over the heads of 862 senior officers and aroused considerable bitterness in military circles. The new general was then returned to the Philippines to remain as military governor until his recall to the States in 1913.

When Pancho Villa's depredations against American citizens and garrisons could no longer be overlooked, President Wilson dispatched General Pershing to "pursue and disperse" the Mexican guerilla band. Upon arriving in El Paso to assemble his troops, Pershing learned that his wife Helen, daughter of United States Senator Warren of Wyoming, and three small daughters had just burned to death in a fire in the quarters of Presidio, Monterey. Only his son Warren survived. Stoically, he went ahead and crossed the border in March, 1916. Amid international tension and complication, improvising supply over impassable trails in hostile country, Pershing moved fast and deep. Villa himself was never caught, but his band of guerillas was dispersed after ten months of pursuit. Pershing was promoted to Major General during the action.

With America's entry into World War I, Pershing was sent to France in the spring of 1917 to command the not yet existent American Expeditionary Force. His job was to create it and then lead it.

While Washington contemplated a limited war, Pershing was laying the foundation for an envisioned vast new land army of three million men and set about with the characteristic skill, energy, and often ruthlessness that had earned him the sobriquet "Black Jack." Aloof and despotic, his only yardstick was efficiency. He was meticulous, too, about training, arming, and equipping his troops before they ever saw combat.

The French wanted to subsume American troops as reinforcements for their own corps, but Pershing refused and stood adamantly for maintaining the integrity of his units. The contentions in this and other areas led constantly to requests for his replacement, but Secretary of War Baker backed him unfailingly. The disasters of early 1918 showed the risks entailed in his efforts, and he put all his forces at Marshal Foch's disposal; but he was vindicated in September when all–United States forces in an all–United States operation defeated the Germans at the St. Mihiel Salient. That was followed by his unrelenting push through the trenches of the Meuse-Argonne, and finally, the victorious completion of the war. He then attended the Paris Peace Conference and the Treaty of Versailles.

Congress in 1919 created for him the rank of general of the armies. This made him the highest ranking officer in United States history. In 1921 he became army chief of staff, before his statutory retirement in July. His decorations included the Distinguished Service Cross, Distinguished Service Medal, Order of the Bath, Légion d'Honneur, Croix de Guerre, medals from Japan, Belgium, Czechoslovakia, Greece, Italy, Montenegro, Panama, Poland, China, Serbia, and Rumania, and a shower of LL.D.'s.

General Pershing served as chairman of the American Battle Monuments Commission and was urged in 1920 and 1924 to become a Presidential candidate, but declined. He published the Pulitzer Prize–winning *My Experiences in the World War* in 1931, and after 1941, lived quietly in quarters built for him at Walter Reed Hospital, where he died July 15, 1948.

Major Walter Reed

(1851–1902)

THE man who was to become recognized as one of the world's greatest bacteriological scientists obtained his two medical degrees while still a teen-ager.

Walter Reed was born in Belroi, Virginia, on September 13, 1851, the youngest of a minister's six children. After completing private school, he entered the University of Virginia in 1867. With one year of academic studies and a year of medicine, he obtained his M.D. in 1869. He then went to New York's Bellevue Hospital and took his second M.D. in 1870, by the time he was nineteen.

He worked for the Board of Health in New York before entering the Army as a lieutenant in 1875. A year later he was married and eventually had a daughter and a son, who grew up to become an infantry officer. Soon Reed was sent to Arizona, and spent eleven years in a frontier garrison before managing a transfer to Baltimore in 1890. Here he studied at Johns Hopkins, became expert in bacteriology, and received promotions and increasingly important appointments.

The outbreak of the Spanish-American War in 1898 saw Major Reed's career spiral upward. Placed in charge of a commission to investigate the epidemic of typhoid fever then raging in United States Army camps, he produced an exhaustive report that was recognized as a permanent landmark in all further studies of typoid epidemiology.

This brilliant and characteristically painstaking work led to his being directed in 1900 to head another commission with an even more challenging task.

General Leonard Wood's troops in Havana were being decimated by yellow fever: a third of his staff officers had already died. It was the commission's job to try to check this plague that made men turn yellow and vomit black before dying painfully.

Reed and his associates, Lazear, Carroll, and Agramonte set up camp outside Havana and got to work. Reasoning that mosquitoes transmitted the disease, they recruited volunteers at $200 apiece and subjected the group, along with Lazear and Carroll, to bites from mosquitoes which had fed upon infected patients. All became infected, though all recovered but Lazear. A control group was housed in mosquito-proof huts, using the befouled clothing and bedding of fever victims. Reed was finally able to establish the *Aëdes aegypti* mosquito as the fever transmitter. War on the deadly insect began immediately under Major W. C. Gorgas, who later used the same methods with great effectiveness and thus helped to assure the completion of the Panama Canal. The results of the seven-month fight, from June, 1900, to February, 1901, were dramatic: in 1900, 1400 cases of yellow fever in Havana alone; in 1901, 37 cases in all Cuba; in 1902, not one.

Upon completion of this project, Reed, a sociable, attractive man known for giving generous credit to the work of his subordinates, returned to Washington to teach at what is now George Washington University. His preoccupation with teaching led him to neglect a chronic appendicitis until a doctor discovered an irreparable condition, and he died under surgery on November 22, 1902. He published some thirty works during his lifetime, and is commemorated by the Army Medical Center's great general hospital in Washington, D.C., which bears his name.

General Philip H. Sheridan
(1831–1888)

As is so often the case in the lives of other military academy graduates, Phil Sheridan's pugnacity and not his scholastic performance seemed to prefigure his eventual succession to high military office. As a West Point cadet, he once broke ranks to accost a superior officer who he thought had treated him unfairly and, with fixed bayonet, chased him off the field. The incident cost him a year's suspension before he won reinstatement, finally graduating in 1853, thirty-fourth in a class of forty-nine.

Philip Henry Sheridan was born in Albany, New York, March 6, 1831, third of six children of Irish immigrants John and Mary Sheridan. His boyhood was spent in rural Ohio, where the family moved shortly after his birth. As a youth, he was keenly disappointed at being too young to enter the Mexican War, but in 1848 he secured entry to West Point through his own efforts.

He rose to captain during Indian fighting on the frontier, then at the outbreak of the Civil War was appointed colonel in charge of the 2nd Michigan Cavalry under Halleck in Tennessee. A month after making colonel, he was promoted to brigadier general of Volunteers for his exemplary conduct during the Battle of Boonville, and by the following December, he was a major general of Volunteers. Sheridan won distinction for his effective support of General Rosecrans in maneuvering Bragg's Confederates out of Tennessee, and then in covering Rosecrans' confused retreat from Chickamauga to Chattanooga.

In subsequent fighting around Chattanooga, his daring charge up and over Missionary Ridge attracted the attention of General Grant, who, upon assuming command of the Army of the Potomac, placed Sheridan in command of his cavalry.

In this capacity, Sheridan proved to be the most able cavalry leader of the war. His corps were active in the battles of the Wilderness, Todd's Tavern, and Spotsylvania Court House, where they disrupted Confederate communications in raids on telegraph and railroad facilities.

August, 1864, saw him charged with the command of the newly formed Army of the Shenandoah, under orders to clear the valley of Confederates. He proved fully equal to the challenge in a brilliant and decisive campaign, defeating General Jubal Early at Winchester and Fisher's Mill. Sheridan then followed his often-censured scorched-earth policy, driving all domestic animals out and leaving civilian inhabitants of the once-fertile area on the verge of starvation. His characteristic justification was that of military necessity, occasioned by the valley's sustaining guerilla forces such as "Mosby's Men" that had for three years dealt defeat after defeat to Union troops.

A few weeks later, on October 19, the new brigadier general of regular Army performed his most famous exploit, acclaimed in poetry and painting as "Sheridan's Ride." His old foe Jubal Early had thrown the main body of Sheridan's army into confusion with a surprise attack at Cedar Creek. Hearing the news when twenty miles away, he swiftly mounted, and arriving upon the scene after a breakneck ride, rallied his troops and turned certain defeat into a stunning victory.

Commissioned a major general in the regular Army, Sheridan then engaged in further successful raids upon enemy communications and supplies; and finally, in April, 1865, he turned General Lee's flank at Five Forks, forcing him to retreat to Appomattox, where he surrendered to General Grant.

In 1867, Sheridan was sent to New Orleans as commander of the Fifth Military District, where his harsh measures in dealing with a conquered South led to disagreements with the more conciliatory President Johnson. He was transferred to head the Department of the Missouri where he successfully campaigned in the Indian War.

Sheridan went to Europe to observe the Franco-Prussian War of 1870, met Bismarck, von Moltke, and his host, the King of Prussia, and witnessed the Battle of Sédan. Three years later he was made chief in command of the United States Army. Not until 1875 did he marry; his bride, Irene, was the daughter of Quartermaster General Rucker. The Sheridans had four children. The last months of his life were spent writing his two-volume *Personal Memoirs*. He signed the preface three days before his death, August 5, 1888, at Nonquitt, Massachusetts, and shortly after his elevation to the rank of full general.

William Howard Taft
(1857–1930)

THE twenty-sixth President of the United States was once unkindly, but accurately, described as "a large good-natured body, entirely surrounded by people who know exactly what they want." His trademarks were a sweeping walrus mustache, a gargantuan, infectious chuckle, an acreage of white linen suiting topped by a floppy-brimmed Panama hat, and an affable tendency toward procrastination and vacillation. Each step upward in his remarkable career he took reluctantly, urged by his more ambitious wife, brother and friends. "Politics," he said, "make me sick."

One of eight children (two of his six brothers died in infancy), Taft was born in Cincinnati on September 15, 1857. His father was an affluent, puritanical judge from New England who later fitted in uneasily as a member of President Grant's cabinet. The family background foreordained him for the law and the Republican party. He was an excellent student, graduating at the head of his class from Yale, and taking his law degree at Cincinnati Law School in 1880.

Taft practiced law and held small political offices until his marriage in 1886 to an attractive, ambitious woman. She bore him a daughter and two sons, one of whom, named Robert Alphonso after his grandfather, became Senator ("Mr. Republican") Taft, of Ohio.

The future President's star began to rise steadily. He ascended the bench (where he was always happiest) in 1887, was appointed Solicitor General in Washington by President Harrison in 1890, made federal circuit court judge in 1892, asked by President McKinley in 1900 to become a member of the Philippine Commission, and, subsequently, civil governor of the Islands, where he proved a sympathetic and efficient administrator, despite marked friction with the military governor, General Arthur MacArthur, father of Douglas.

In 1904, Taft was recalled by President Roosevelt to become Secretary of War, a post he filled with vigor, pushing construction of the Panama Canal, trouble-shooting in general, and earning high favor with Roosevelt, who finally offered Taft as his hand-picked candidate for the Presidency in 1908.

After defeating William Jennings Bryan handily, Taft spent what were undoubtedly four of the unhappiest years of his life, in the White House. Saddled with a weak cabinet, insurgents in his own party, and growing Democratic strength, he found that the public popularity he so cherished had slipped away from him. Although he actually did more trust-busting than Roosevelt, he was denounced as a reactionary enemy of labor. Contemporary historians called him the worst failure since Grant. Given the political climate of the day, however, it is unlikely that any Republican President would have fared much better.

After the 1912 election, when he received the pitiful eight electoral votes of Utah and Vermont, Taft gladly left Washington to become Kent Professor of Law at Yale. Here he remained until 1921 when President Harding granted him his heart's desire by naming him Chief Justice of the Supreme Court. Presiding over the court, whose members included Louis Brandeis and Oliver Wendell Holmes, Taft's legal views, as always, displayed his conservatism, with little disposition to dissent; a sound legal mind; and solid integrity.

This last and happiest office he held until he resigned with a heart ailment on February 3, 1930. He died a short time later, on March 8.

General Jonathan M. Wainwright

(1883–1953)

WHEN General MacArthur made his celebrated PT-boat dash from the Philippines in March, 1942, he left the beleaguered island forces in command of "Skinny" Wainwright who was, he said, "a modern warrior with enough horse-soldier tradition to hold that line if it can be held." The line, it turned out, could not be held, and was swamped by overwhelming Japanese forces.

Newly promoted to major general, Wainwright had been ordered to the Philippines in 1940, grumbling that "something might break, and there I'd be in the Philippines, missing everything." After the attack on Pearl Harbor he directed well-trained American and Filipino troops in the viciously fought but losing Bataan Peninsula campaign against the Japanese. Hounded at last to the small, rocky island of Corregidor, Wainwright huddled with several thousand tatterdemalion men and nurses under ceaseless enemy bombardment that reached an intensity of a barrage of 500-pound shells every five seconds for hours on end. Finally, at the end of food and equipment, Wainwright surrendered all his forces to General Yamashita in May 6, 1942. As he had earlier vowed, he went into captivity with his men and was finally sent to a prison camp in Manchuria. There, along with British General Percival of Singapore, he was consistently humiliated in an unsuccessful attempt to make him "lose face." At the risk of his own safety Wainwright frequently intervened in the mistreatment of his men. He was freed by American parachutists in time for the sweet chore of accepting the surrender of General Yamashita aboard the *Missouri* in 1945. Upon his release Wainwright said he was afraid the American people would not forgive him for surrendering his forces on Corregidor. He need not have worried. Later that year he was awarded the Congressional Medal of Honor for his "intrepid leadership" during his heroic stand.

There is the clank and rattle of saber and spur to everything about the life of Jonathan Mayhew Wainwright before "Saddle up!" gave way to "Roll 'em!" The great-grandson of a prominent Episcopalian bishop, and grandson of a Civil War commander killed in battle, he was their namesake and later perpetuated the name through his son. He was born on August 23, 1883, in Walla Walla, Washington, to Major Robert Powell Page Wainwright, who commanded a cavalry squadron in the Battle of Santiago and later was killed in action during the Philippine Insurrection of 1901. The boy grew up in posts on the frontier where his father had fought Indians. Like his father, he attended West Point and graduated in 1906, having acquired his nickname and a commission as second lieutenant of cavalry. For two years he rode with various outfits in Texas, then went to fight the Moros in the Philippines in 1909. The next several years were spent with the cavalry's rifle team and its mounted service school, and by World War I he was a captain seeing action in the Saint-Mihiel and Meuse-Argonne offensives. After the armistice, his brilliant staff work with the Third Army, in Germany, won him the Distinguished Service Medal.

In 1920 he made major and eight years later he was relieved of general staff duty and "for the next six years buckled down to studying for the next war." He graduated from the Command and General Staff School in 1931 and the War College in 1934. Promotions were steady and in 1938 he became a brigadier general in command of the First Cavalry Brigade.

After the war, Wainwright returned to the United States to a hero's welcome and a brief post on Governor's Island before going, in 1946, to Fort Sam Houston at San Antonio as commander of the Fourth Army. That same year, he brought out his autobiography, *General Wainwright's Story,* edited by Bob Considine. Following his retirement in 1947, he became an insurance company executive and devoted his time to business interests. He died of a stroke on September 2, 1953, in Brooke Army Hospital at Fort Sam Houston.

This "typical, long, lean cavalryman who loved a fine horse" was said to be heartbroken at the advent of tanks because, being bowlegged, he fit a horse so much better. The official War Department biography carried the capsule description, "Natural leader, magnetic personality, clipped speech, good disciplinarian, popular with officers and men, alert, forceful. Plenty of confidence in himself."

ARLINGTON NAT

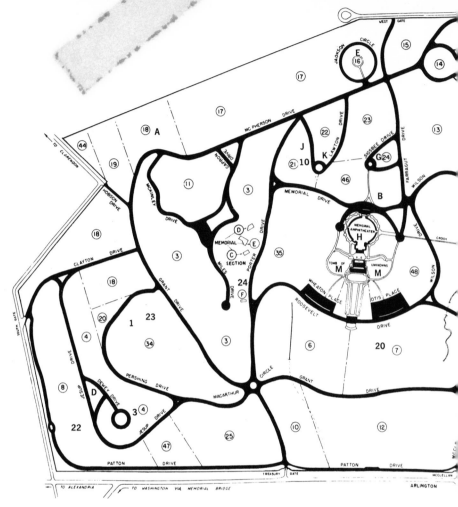

KEY

	Section and Grave Numbers		
1—General Henry H. Arnold	34-44A	14—Chief Justice Oliver Wendell Holmes	5-7004
2—Stephen Vincent Benét	1-154	15—General Philip Kearny	2
3—William Jennings Bryan	4-3121	16—John Fitzgerald Kennedy	45
4—Admiral Richard E. Byrd	2-4969	17—Admiral William D. Leahy	2-932
5—General Claire Chennault	2-873	18—Major Pierre Charles L'Enfant	2
6—General John Clem	2-993	19—Robert Todd Lincoln	31
7—General George Crook	2-974	20—General George C. Marshall	7-8198
8—General Willam Donovan	2-4874	21—Admiral Marc Mitscher	2-4942
9—Abner Doubleday	1-61	22—Robert E. Peary	8
10—John Foster Dulles	21-31	23—General John J. Pershing	34-1
11—Medgar Evers	36-1431	24—Major Walter Reed	3-1864
12—James V. Forrestal	30-674	25—General Philip H. Sheridan	2
13—Admiral William F. Halsey, Jr.	2-1184	26—William Howard Taft	30-S-14
		27—General Jonathan M. Wainwright	1-358